THE EDINBURGH HIGHLAND REEL
AND STRATHSPEY SOCIETY

THE EDINBURGH HIGHLAND REEL AND STRATHSPEY SOCIETY
A History

James Moray Calder

EDITED BY GEORGE A. ROBERTSON

TUCKWELL PRESS
EAST LINTON, SCOTLAND
www.tuckwellpress.co.uk

First published in Great Britain in 2001 by
Tuckwell Press
The Mill House
Phantassie
East Linton
East Lothian EH40 3DG
Scotland

ISBN 1 86232 144 2

British Library Cataloguing in Publication Data

A catalogue record for this book is available
on request from the British Library

Typeset by Hewer Text Ltd, Edinburgh
Printed and bound by Bell and Bain Ltd, Glasgow

This book is dedicated to all who love the native music of Scotland

Contents

List of Illustrations

Foreword

The Edinburgh Highland Reel and Strathspey Society, the first of its kind, was formed in 1881 'for the practice or promotion of Scottish National Music, more especially Reel and Strathspey playing in the old Highland fashion'. The institution of the Society and the practice facilities resulted from a meeting, attended by, amongst others, a trio of kindred spirits – 'brethren of the bow' – William Simpson, who became Leader of the Orchestra in 1885, and was in the employment of the Highland Society (now the Royal Highland & Agricultural Society of Scotland); James Stewart Robertson of Edradynate, who was the Society's first President and who compiled the *Athole Collection*; and Archibald Menzies, S.S.C., who was the Society's first Secretary and Conductor.

From the early days, small groups of fiddlers from the Orchestra have assisted at innumerable small concerts etc. arranged by Churches and charitable bodies for social purposes and the raising of funds. In addition to the annual Concerts, many others have been held in the Usher Hall, such as Fiddlers' Rallies, concerts featuring regimental bands, the International Gathering of the Clans, etc.

From the inception of the Orchestra until 1949, its composition was violins (first and second), violas, 'cellos and double basses. Thereafter the piano was introduced. In the early days the music played by the Orchestra was the strathspeys and reels as contained in the *Athole Collection* and the other publications available at that time, together with Scots airs. With the great interest in Scottish country dancing which occurred after 1945, the Society extended their repertoire to include sets of country dances arranged by John Robertson and James M. Calder who were associated, in succession, with the Scottish Country Dance Players and the Scottish Country Players who broadcast regularly on BBC Radio.

Archibald Menzies was appointed Conductor in 1889. He continued, with considerable enthusiasm, to promote the interests of the

Society until his death in 1914. He was succeeded by his son, Ian C. Menzies, who, until his death in 1949, carried on the fine traditions set by his father. James M. Calder was appointed as his successor, having joined the Orchestra in 1931, playing violin and thereafter, double bass to help that section of the Orchestra. He retired from office in 1991. The Orchestra of the Society is presently under the baton of Jim Ferguson.

The Society is in a very strong position, being under able leadership and with an extended library of Scottish music. The playing season extends from October to March. Membership is open to performers on the violin, viola, 'cello and double bass.

Editor's Preface

When James M. Calder died suddenly in November 1999, much of this history was complete but a few gaps remained. Further material has been added by Hamish Calder, the author's son.

The Society gave me the task of editing and preparing the text, which I willingly accepted. In the course of going over James M. Calder's manuscript I have deleted, amended or added material as I thought necessary. I hope that in no place has this affected the sense or significance of what he wrote.

I wish to thank all who gave help, encouragement, and assistance as work progressed on this project, in particular the Calder family who, for the last century, have dedicated much of their lives to the running and wellbeing of the Society.

Grateful thanks are also due to all past and present members of the Society without whom there would be no history.

George A. Robertson
June 2001

Introduction

I have the qualification of a long association with the Society in a variety of ways. My father, Alexander S. Calder, who came to Edinburgh from Forres, Morayshire, as a young man, joined the Society in 1902. His father, James Calder, as reported by the local press on his death,

> was a great lover of the violin and figured frequently at the head of local orchestras on festive occasions, his services in that capacity being much appreciated. – He was in great demand at country dances, and could handle the violin bow with great zest.

This love of Scottish music passed to my father who was invited to become Secretary of the Society and was elected to that office in 1903. He continued as Secretary for the rest of his life. While I became a playing member in 1931, I had already attended many practice meetings and Annual Concerts. I can recall the Monday evening meetings in the Highland Society of Scotland's rooms in George IV Bridge, Edinburgh. The fiddlers sat round the very large boardroom table with their music books on desk stands placed thereon, with the Conductor, Ian C. Menzies, at the top of the table. The music was played with great enthusiasm.

The format of the practice meetings seldom varied. The practice commenced at 8.00pm with the playing of one of the many sets of strathspeys and reels which constituted the main part of the Library of the Orchestra. Each set consisted of three strathspeys and three reels played alternately – strathspey: reel; strathspey: reel; strathspey; reel. The Conductor indicated the start of a set in the usual way. Thereafter each tune was played at the appropriate speed and repeated two, three or four times until he was satisfied that the somewhat unsteady and perhaps inaccurate playing had settled down to a reasonably accurate version of the tune. Only at this stage did he indicate by a wave of his baton that the players should proceed to the next tune in the set. The same procedure was adopted for this and remaining tunes. The playing of a set was indeed a somewhat tiring exercise. The playing of further sets together with a set of Scots airs continued to 10.00pm or thereby. It was not unusual for several of the older members to ask to be excused at around 9.45pm, ostensibly to be in time for a tramcar. The fact that the local pub closed at 10.00pm was perhaps a coincidence!

In terms of the Rules of the Society, I was tested by the Conductor and Leader who were satisfied that I had the required playing skills to be admitted as a Playing Member. It was not long before I realised that the playing of strathspeys and reels requires something more than the ability to play scales and arpeggios and sight-read in a modest way. My experience of my first dozen or so practice meetings made clear to me that speed of execution was very necessary for effective playing. I became the Conductor of the orchestra in 1949 and was privileged to hold that position for 42 years until retirement in 1991.

I am grateful for the support and loyalty shown to the Society by members over many years in turning out for practices and performing at their best during the concerts. It has been my good fortune to be able to arrange music for the orchestra, to conduct its performance and to hear it played. I am also grateful for the valuable assistance given by those who helped the Society in so many different ways, particularly in making arrangements for the concerts and looking after the Society's music.

The Society has always sought to be outward-looking and to pass on a love of Scottish music to as wide an audience as possible. The Annual Concerts have been the most visible way of doing this but much encouragement has also been given to fellow societies throughout Scotland. I am also proud that the Society's important tradition of helping charities by raising funds with its music has continued and expanded.

All societies have a social side and this one is no exception. Friendships and even romance have blossomed amongst members brought together by a shared interest. The Annual Dinner, the Social Evenings, the Competitions and the Golf Club have all had an important part to play.

It is remarkable that the Society has been able to carry on actively throughout such a long period, given the many social and other changes that have taken place. This is due entirely to the keenness of the playing members. That the Society had only three Conductors over a period of more than 100 years undoubtedly helped preserve its continuity and traditions. Nevertheless the Society has not been slow to play new music and arrangements and to move with the times. I have now laid down my baton and it is for others to take the Society forward into a new century. I wish them every success in doing so.

James M. Calder
Edinburgh
November 1999

CHAPTER ONE

1881

Of the many gentlemen whose enthusiasm for and interest in traditional Scottish music led to the formation of the Edinburgh Highland Reel and Strathspey Society, the first and foremost was William Simpson.

He published, for private circulation, a booklet entitled *A Spring on the Fiddle*. He opens with these words:

There is nothing more cheerful than a spring on the fiddle. It is fully enjoyed by all in town or country, more especially about Christmas, when the evenings are long and often dull. It is then many dance-parties are given to while away the long dreary nights, the memory of which does not die down in after years. We often hear of such gatherings taking place in distant parts of the world in commemoration of those held at home. It is quite refreshing receiving letters from abroad giving such reports. The fiddle is greatly played by our farm men in the North. They usually play strathspeys and reels very well, with a fine crisp stroke. I should say in all fairness that those men I have met in the North are particularly good with a well-measured length of bow. I had the satisfaction in early life of meeting a few who were exceptionally good, and I could name a few who may be remembered by some still living. I am speaking away back in 1860–1–2–3. I was at the time living in the vicinity of Elgin (Morayshire). At that time the great Volunteer movement was in full swing, companies being formed all over the country, the band usually being a few flutes and drums, &c. Mr Peter Milne, a well-known fiddler from Aberdeen, came to Elgin at that time, and played a piccolo-flute with the Volunteer band. Having got the fiddle craze, I put myself under his tuition, and got very useful lessons.

William Simpson, in 1863, went to Ireland where he stayed for about six years in Co. Galway, then on to Tipperary. There he met some very fine jig players. On leaving Ireland in 1869, he went to Perthshire, Aberfeldy district. In his words:

> Here I again came in contact with many fine reel players, among whom was Wm. M'Leish, whom I was under for some years. Then at Dunkeld we had M'Kerchar and the M'Intoshes, who are still there. Mr J. Stewart Robertson, Sir R. Menzies (cello), Major Craigie, and Mr Charles Paterson were also all very keen players.

The Gold Medal subsequently given to the Society for annual competition by Charles Paterson is referred to in the next chapter.

The narrative continues:

> Having renewed the acquaintance of Mr Stewart Robertson of Edradynate, when I came to live in Edinburgh I found he was staying for the winter in Heriot Row. I met him frequently, and as usual the violin and reels were usually discussed. I informed him that I had met a great many reel players since I came to stay in Edinburgh, and some were very fine players, and he seemed rather interested. I mentioned where I met them, and pointed out the unfavourable conditions of having a pleasant time together, and suggested that a Society or club might be formed. He did not quite fall in with me at the time, but after a few meetings he and I had over the matter, he suggested that a meeting with a few representatives might be held, to which I agreed. Next day he called on me at the Highland Society's Rooms, and after talking the matter over he said, 'What can you do with those fellows?' I said the whole thing was quite simple. A meeting was arranged to be held at 3 George IV. Bridge, but on the morning of the meeting I had a note from him saying he would prefer St Andrew Square, to save him coming up the Mound, which I agreed to, and the meeting was held in Mr Menzies' office.

William Simpson's booklet, *A Spring on the Fiddle*, takes us behind the scenes with regard to the early meetings of the enthusiasts who wished to form the Association which emerged as the Edinburgh Highland Reel and Strathspey Society. The early records of the Society are contained in well-kept Minute Books. The first formal minute begins as follows:

Minutes of Meeting of gentlemen desirous of forming an association for the practice or promotion of Scottish National Music, more especially Reel and Strathspey playing in the old Highland fashion, held at 7 St. Andrew Square, Edin on Saturday, the 26th March 1881, at 2 o'clock P.M.

Present
Mr J. Stewart Robertson of Edradynate
Mr W. Simpson, 3 George IV Bridge
Mr Rob Watson, 85 Rosemount Bldgs
Mr W. Fraser, 3 Heriot Mount &
Mr A. Menzies.

Mr Stewart Robertson was called to the chair – Mr A. Menzies acted as Secretary pro tem.

The Secretary intimated to the meeting the purposes for which it was called, namely, to consider the advisability of forming a Society in Edinburgh for the upholding and developing the taste for our old national highland strathspey and reel music on the violin.

The chairman, in supporting the idea, said that it was very desirable that this class of music should not be allowed to fall back as undoubtedly it was doing for the past few years.

William Simpson informs us: 'Little was done at that meeting, and no end of difficulties arose on many points. Several meetings were held with little or no work done, as there was no money to get music or stands, and any possibility of a start being made was very remote'. At the second meeting concerning the formation of a Reel and Strathspey Society, again held at St. Andrew Square, Edinburgh, on 5 April 1881, there were present those who had attended the first meeting with the addition of W. Hay, 23 Orwell Place, Thomas Gilbert, 10 Warriston Crescent, and John Hardie and Charles Hardie, both of 10 Clyde Street.

The meeting considered that it was necessary in order to form the Society at once that office bearers be appointed. Archibald Menzies moved that James Stewart Robertson be appointed President of the Society, as, in his opinion, no more suitable gentleman could be got in Scotland for the post. This was unanimously agreed. Archibald Menzies was then appointed Secretary and Treasurer *pro tem.* Robert Watson was appointed Librarian. The appointment of a conductor and a leader was, in the meantime, left in abeyance. Three ordinary members – Messrs Simpson, Fraser and Gilbert – were elected as members of the committee.

It was further agreed that in order to be able to commence practice at the earliest possible date the President should use his influence with the Highland and Agricultural Society, through their Secretary, Fletcher Norton Menzies, to allow the use of the rooms in the Highland Society's premises at 3 George IV Bridge for practice. One of the original objects of the Highland and Agricultural Society of Scotland, as defined at the meeting held on 11 January 1785, was that 'The Society shall also pay a proper attention to the preservation of the language, poetry and music of the Highlands'.

William Simpson tells a slightly different story:

> Just at that time, when matters seemed against us, a Mr Ramsay of the *Banffshire Journal* came to write up the History of the Highland and Agricultural Society, and on turning out all the old documents we came on a report giving the early doings of the Society, when that body sent Captain Simon Fraser through the Highlands to collect all songs and music that were unpublished at the time. On seeing this report I got Mr Fletcher Norton Menzies, who was then Secretary of the Highland and Agricultural Society, to ask the Directors for the use of their hall for practice.

The meetings held on 26 March and 5 April 1881 were attended by gentlemen who were keen to form a Reel and Strathspey Society. At the second meeting, although the draft Rules and Byelaws had not been adjusted and finalised, Office Bearers had been appointed so that at the next meeting on Tuesday, 12 April 1881, held at the Highland Society's rooms at 3 George IV Bridge, attended by 'members of the Edinburgh Highland Reel and Strathspey Society', the Society formally came into existence.

The main requirement of the Society at this time was a suitable place for practice meetings. At the above meeting, the President intimated that the Highland Society had kindly granted the use of one of their rooms for the purpose of practice, at least during the remainder of the session which was about to close. The minutes record: 'They were thus enabled to hold their first meeting for practice and the members afterwards joined in practice of Highland Reels and Strathspeys'. The privilege of holding practice meetings in that hall was enjoyed until the Highland and Agricultural Society moved to new premises in Eglinton Crescent in 1928.

There was a further meeting of the members of the Society on 30 September 1881 when some discussion took place on the subject of subscriptions and entry money and the like. It was agreed to submit the various proposals to the Annual General Meeting, to be held on Tuesday, 4 October 1881.

The minutes of meeting of the members of the Society, held on Tuesday, 4 October 1881, record that this was the first General Meeting. The Chairman intimated that the use of the Highland Society's rooms had been granted and the Society would meet during this session for practice. Considerable discussion took place regarding the amount of subscription and entry money for ordinary and life members. These were ultimately agreed at 5/- (£0.25) as the annual subscription and the like sum for entry money. Life members would also pay entry money of 5/- (£0.25) and a life subscription of £2.2/- (£2.10). The business of the meeting being concluded, the members then engaged in reels and strathspeys.

William Simpson, proceeding with his narration of the early days of the Society, writes:

Things were very flat for a bit. Mr M'Intyre was appointed the leader, which he held for a year or so, but as matters were not very encouraging, he, being a professional player, resigned. The usual attendance per night was six to eight in all. The names of those were Fraser, Shearlaw, Gunn, Simpson, M'Intyre, Hardie, and a little later on Messrs Laidlaw, Greenshield, Farquhar, A. Patterson, the Gerards (James, William, John, and Alexander), and R. Watson. Mr William Gerard, sen., was a very keen player and regular attender; also J. Logan, M'Allan, O. Logan, D. Gunn. Before this Mr A. Menzies had won the Queen's Prize, and having an appointment in the Volunteers at Headquarters, was prevented from being oftener with us.

Before closing his report on the early days of the Society, William Simpson sets out his view on the lack of interest in our national music and the reason for the renaissance in which the Society took an early and leading part:

> At the time the Highland Reel and Strathspey Society came into existence, Scottish music had fallen to a very low ebb in Edinburgh. Time was when ball programmes contained a goodly number of Scottish dances – such as reels, country dances, Reel of Tulloch, &c. – but often when these were reached they were changed for waltzes in preference. It was either the company were too lazy, or that these required more skill than they had at their command. Much the same thing happened with Scottish songs – you would hardly meet any one who could sing them unless very good professionals. The country was overrun with Germans and other foreign teachers, who would not or could not either sing or play Scottish music. To hear the best of them make the attempt is a thing not to be forgotten by those who know better.
>
> It is quite refreshing now to find the changes that have come over the people – they are now learning all the Highland dances.

It will be seen from the foregoing narrative and excerpts from minutes of meetings that the Society came into being as a result of the meeting together of a trio of kindred spirits, 'brethren of the bow': William Simpson, James Stewart Robertson and Archibald Menzies, along with the other enthusiasts who are mentioned by name. The other essential element was the association with and kind co-operation of the Highland and Agricultural Society of Scotland. One of the conditions on which that Society was granted its charter was that it would encourage the study of Highland poetry and the practice of Highland music.

CHAPTER TWO

1882–1901

The early practice meetings of the fiddlers were held on Tuesday evenings. At a meeting of the members of the Society held on Saturday, 18 March 1882, specially convened, it was agreed that the meeting night should be changed to Monday, as it was thought that this might suit a greater number of members. While membership had been increasing, the attendance of playing members at practice meetings had declined. Apart from war years, Monday has remained the practice evening.

It is clear from the records that considerable interest in the playing of strathspeys and reels was being taken by Honorary Members and friends who were in the habit of attending the practice meetings.

The room used for practice at 3 George IV Bridge was clearly not large enough for the audience. The minute of 3 April 1882 records that the meeting commenced at 10.00pm, after the practice meeting. It was agreed 'that it would be necessary in future to enable the practices to be carried out satisfactorily that the number of outside visitors should be restricted and that only one night a month should be open for visitors'. Accordingly, only playing members were entitled to admission to the weekly practices of the Society except on the first meeting night in each month, which would be open to visitors.

After the practice meeting on 17 April 1882, the Rules of the Society were again discussed when various matters – the calling of meetings, borrowing of music etc. – were the main topics. Eventually, it was deputed to the President and the Secretary to have the Rules adjusted, written out and signed.

Even among musicians there may be discord! The minute of the meeting held on 12 February 1883 discloses that it was called 'for the consideration of the circumstances attending the misunderstanding existing between two of the members of the Society viz. Mr R Watson and Mr John Hardie'. The meeting resolved that in respect of the personal remarks made by John Hardie and his conduct towards Robert

Watson at a recent practice that John Hardie be debarred from attending the meetings of the Society until he should amply apologise to Robert Watson and the Society by letter addressed through the Secretary and that should he fail to do so, he be expelled from the Society. The resolution was communicated to John Hardie who replied by letter declaring it his intention to abide by the decision of the Society, and refusing to apologise.

The records of the early years of the Society indicate that the Society was being run without any substantial funds. The first account submitted, from the date of formation to 30 September 1882, showed an income of £9–9/- (£9.45) and an expenditure of £6–7/- (£6.35), leaving a balance of £3–2/- (£3.10). The following year, to 30 September 1883, showed a deficiency of 2/7 (£0.13). After outstanding payments, the funds at credit amounted to £1–15–5 (£1.77). During this early period, the playing membership increased with many new members being proposed and admitted. At this time, all prospective playing members were examined so that a good standard of playing might be maintained. The minute of the Annual General Meeting held on 8 October 1883 reports that William Laidlaw, 5 North St. James Street was so examined. It was fortunate for the Society that he passed the test! William Simpson's long connection with the Society was brought to an end by his death on 6 October 1920. William Laidlaw was elected leader in his place and thereafter worthily served the Society in that capacity for the next 28 years.

In addition to fiddlers, a number of double bass players were also recruited. A wider membership was sought and, to this end, the Secretary, in his Annual Report to the Annual General Meeting on 8 October 1883, stated that a circular had been recently issued regarding the Society and widely distributed among the nobility and gentry of Scotland, which it was anticipated would add significantly to the membership.

This circular setting forth the aims of the Society did not immediately produce the result intended. It was reported to the members at a meeting on 28 January 1884 that 'a very few indeed had responded, but notwithstanding this the membership was increasing through the private efforts of the members'.

One of the tasks facing the committee in these early years was the provision of music for the players. There were available various printed collections containing strathspeys and reels, jigs and slow airs. The Society had insufficient funds to purchase such music. Further, music in book form was not well suited to a group of players.

The Society were deeply grateful to their President, James Stewart Robertson of Cluny and Edradynate, Strathtay when he presented the two volumes of the *Athole Collection*, his compilation of strathspeys and reels, published in December 1883. He also offered to instruct the publishers, if the Society wished to use the *Athole Collection* for practices, to supply a further six copies at cost price. The Society were pleased to accept the liberality and kindness of their President to whom the best thanks of the Society were conveyed. Although the funds of the Society were not sufficiently flourishing to defray the cost, six copies were ordered for immediate use. It was agreed that there should be a levy on members for an extra subscription.

James Stewart Robertson, as was usual at this time, published his collection for subscribers. While he makes reference to the collection being the work of an amateur, it was a monumental achievement of a dedicated Scotsman who thereby rendered a great service to his native land.

Almost three years from the first informal playing of strathspeys and reels in the rooms of the Highland Society, a concert was held there on Monday, 24 March 1884. This was something of a private event for members and their friends. Selections of Strathspeys and Reels were featured, with variety provided by songs in English and Gaelic, and other items including bagpipe selections.

Following a surplus of £8–12/- (£8.60), a further concert was held on 29 April 1884, which like the first was well patronised and much appreciated. This second concert did little more than clear itself as rent was paid for the Freemasons' Hall, and various outlays – advertising, transport of music stands and double basses etc. – were incurred.

On 14 October 1884, the Secretary of the Society wrote to Fletcher Norton Menzies, Secretary of the Highland Society, asking if the privilege of using their hall for practices and concerts could continue. The letter of 5 November 1884 in reply was in favourable terms. The privilege was twofold in that it also allowed the hall for the holding of concerts 'under certain restrictions, viz. that they are to a certain extent *private*, that is, not advertised and that the number of tickets issued for cash, concert and others, not exceed 200'.

The Society were now in a position to hold concerts with the minimum of outlays. A further concert was given in the hall at 3 George IV Bridge on 31 March 1885. The records indicate that

> the success of this concert was quite marked and can only be attributed to the increasing popularity of the Society, and its object: viz. the practice of the National dance music of Scotland. Owing to the limited accommodation of the hall and the consequently limited number of tickets, many were unable during some days before the concert to procure tickets of admission.

With the funds available from this concert, a double bass was purchased at a cost of £4. Encouraged by this success, it was agreed at the beginning of the 1885–86 session that two concerts should be held, one in the beginning of January and one to finish the session in April. The Secretary reported that with this in view some sets had already been arranged, so the Orchestra could enter, at once and with spirit, into the practice for the first concert.

William Simpson was appointed Leader in 1885. He immediately set to work to recruit members, which he was very successful in doing. The want of money was a serious consideration, as a good quantity of music was required. He set about making copies of the music contained in the few books which were available in the Society's library.

The enthusiasm for the playing of reels and strathspeys continued unabated. In February 1886, the committee decided that the programme for the forthcoming concert should include at least six sets, each of three strathspeys and three reels. This pattern was followed for very many years thereafter.

As a result of a successful concert, several gentlemen who were present intimated their intention of becoming honorary members. At the Annual General Meeting on 4 October 1886, the Treasurer reported a balance at credit of the Society of £9–9–8 (£9.48) besides the double bass, music stands, and music. That the Society was finding favour is borne out by the fact that no fewer than thirteen new members were enrolled in the months following. Double bass players were also enrolled to assist at practices and concerts. It was decided that the Society should acquire instruments for their use as the expense of hiring cabs for transport would be saved. In November 1886, the sum of £5 was paid for a good quality instrument, including bag, bow and strings. In the following year, the double basses and other assets were insured for £50.

As at 8 October 1888, the membership stood at 30 Ordinary (playing) members and 23 Honorary members. The size of the Orchestra must have been giving some concern, as, at a meeting of committee some months earlier, it had been suggested that the number of playing members be restricted to 30. This may have been on account of the shortage of music books. Eight further volumes of the *Athole Collection* were purchased at a cost of £1 each. The limiting of the number of playing members was not further discussed. The Secretary, in his Annual Report on the 1887–88 Session, referring to the enthusiastic reception given to the reel playing at the recent concert, suggested that the Society was on the high road to fame, 'and by continued persever-ance it may yet come to make Scotland ring with Strathspeys and Reels from John O'Groats to the Tweed'. To quote from *A Spring on the Fiddle*:

> From this time onwards the Society began to grow in numbers and popularity. Mr A. Menzies was appointed conductor about eight years after the formation of the Society, the numbers being so great that it was considered advisable to have a conductor.

At the Annual General Meeting held on 7 October 1889 Archibald Menzies was elected conductor. This post he held until his death in 1914.

The Secretary, in his Report on the 1889–90 Session, reported that the Orchestra

> had the unusual opportunity of displaying their abilities before one of the largest audiences that ever assembled within the walls of a hall in the City of Edinburgh. Two performances were given on the 9th August last by the members of the Society in the Grand

Hall of the Edinburgh International Exhibition before record audiences, who enthusiastically greeted the rendering of some of our best National Strathspeys and Reels with unbounded applause and from the varied Nationalities assembled there, no doubt the fame of the Edinburgh Highland Reel and Strathspey Society will be established and extended not only from Lands End to John O'Groats but throughout the whole Continent of Europe.

It was decided to commemorate the 10th Anniversary of the Society by having a dinner on 13 April 1891. However, a week or so before the event, on account of the death of a daughter of James Stewart Robertson, the projected dinner was postponed.

In the summer of 1891 the members of the Society met to consider having a picnic. But after some careful consideration and discussion this idea was abandoned, 'and instead of a pic-nic it was suggested by Mr William Simpson that a competition in Strathspey, Reel and Slow Scottish Air playing should be held and be open to all who had been playing members during the session 1890–91'. So, to commemorate the 10th Anniversary, instead of a dinner the Society decided on a competition, which was held on 30 November 1891:

> There were 32 competitors entered for the various sections and classes. The judges were Mr Strachan of Edinburgh, Mr Marshall of Dundee and Mr Work of Glasgow, whose awards to the successful parties were received with unbiased satisfaction. The committee voted a sum of £10 from the Society's funds towards supplying silver medals and other prizes for the competition. The following valuable prizes were also most liberally presented by friends and members of the Society, viz.

> Copy of *Athole Collection* of Strathspeys and Reels by James Stewart Robertson,
> Violin Case by Archibald Menzies,
> Volume of Strathspeys and Reels by William Simpson,
> Silver Medal by Thomas Gilbert,
> Volume of Songs by W. A. G. Brodie,
> 2 Volumes of Reels by Roy Paterson,
> Violin Bow by James Hardie,

Silver Medal by James Brown,
Volume of Strathspeys and Reels by James White.
The Society furnished 4 silver medals, 2 Volumes of Strathspeys
and Reels, and 2 Violin Cases.

The following is the list of successful prize winners, viz.

Section 1,
Class 1, for experienced players, for which there were 4 prizes.
1st Prize, Silver Medal, awarded to James Hardie
2nd Prize, Silver Medal, awarded to Robert Watson
3rd Prize, Volume of Reels, awarded to Archibald Menzies
4th Prize, Volume of Songs, awarded to George Lowe

Class 2, for less experienced players, for which there were 4 prizes.
1st Prize, Silver Medal, awarded to Andrew Fairgrieve
2nd Prize, Violin Case, awarded to James Gerard
3rd Prize, Volume of Reels, awarded to John Logan
4th Prize, Volume of Reels, awarded to Alexander Ormiston

Class 3, for junior members, for which there were 4 prizes.
1st Prize, Silver Medal, awarded to James Dickson
2nd Prize, Violin Case, awarded to Thomas Stewart
3rd Prize, Volume of Reels, awarded to John Shearer
4th Prize, Volume of Reels, awarded to James Brown

Section 2
Class 1, for Strathspey and Hullichan, for which there were 3
prizes.
1st Prize, Copy of *Athole Collection*, awarded to William Simpson
2nd Prize, Silver Medal, awarded to Robert Watson
3rd Prize, Volume of Strathspeys and Reels, awarded to Alexander
Ormiston

Class 2, for Slow Strathspey, for which there were 2 prizes.
1st Prize, Silver Medal, awarded to Archibald Menzies
2nd Prize, Violin Bow, awarded to James Hardie

Class 3, for Solo Scottish Air, for which there were 2 prizes.
1st Prize, Violin Case, awarded to Henry J. Staples
2nd Prize, Volume of Strathspeys and Reels, awarded to Archibald Menzies

It is amusing to see James Hardie, the famous fiddle maker, win his own violin bow for 2nd prize in the Slow Strathspey competition. Born in 1836, he joined the Society in 1888 as a life member, and died in 1916.

A social dinner was eventually held on 25 April 1892. James Stewart Robertson proposed the toast of the Society and said 'That at no time within his knowledge did that class of music appear to be better understood, or more widely appreciated, than at the present time. For that excellent and satisfactory state of matters they were largely indebted to the efforts and work of the Edinburgh Highland Reel and Strathspey Society'.

At the third annual dinner, which was held on 30 April 1894, the minute book informs us:

> On due justice being done to the beverages – a topical song composed specially for the occasion and sung by our Bard, Mr Robert Watson, describing in glowing terms, the sublime quali-fications of the various officials of the Society, created no small amount of amusement.

Here is the very song, evidently to the old tune *Killiecrankie*.

Wha hasna heard the news that's gaun
Mong Fiddlers o' Strathspeys, man,
About their Competitions grand
For Reels and Scottish Lays, man,
 Though some their Reels play far ower quick,
 Yet ithers play gey tardy;
 But Menzies says (an' he should ken),
 That nane can play like Hardie.

Noo, Hardie's an auld-farrent chiel,
Bred far up i' the north, man;
An' Menzies he's o' Heilan' bluid,
Frae far ayont the Forth, man.

Noo, Menzies says, though a' played weel
Yet he wad ne'er be tardy,
Whane' er he had a chance, tae gi'e
The first prize to auld Hardie.

But yet there's lots o' folks we ken,
Wha play Strathspeys fu' weel, man,
Wha werna bred in Heilant glen
And yet can play a reel, man;
But Menzies caresna for their style,
They're ower quick or tardy,
Altho' in Reel o' Tulloch, nane
Played oot o' time like Hardie.

Noo, Simpson, Watson an' the lave
May a' lay by the bow, man,
For what the Major says is backed
By Gilbert an' by Lowe, man.
An' Menzies he micht take a hint
That's gien by a puir bardie,
An' hand the baton tae his frien',
The veteran Jamie Hardie.

Noo, folks may their opeenions change,
But facts they winna budge, man;
An' Menzies, though a lawyer keen,
Was ne'er meant for a Judge, man.
Noo, if a Challenge he should think
Tae gi'e, I'd ne'er be tardy
Tae play a' night Strathspeys an' Reels
Wi' aither him or Hardie.

In addition to the annual dinners the members of the Society held social evenings or 'Smoking Concerts', where it is recorded the evening 'was spent with solos, song and sentiment'. The main object of the Smoking Concert was to enable the playing members to meet together at informal social gatherings and thus become better known to each other, and so promote and strengthen good feeling among the members.

The 14th Annual Report submitted at the Annual General Meeting, held on 7 October 1895, states: 'This year's concert far eclipsed any former performances of the Society, in the manner of precision, expression and uniform style of bowing'. One fact, which no doubt helped to secure these objects, was the appearance of Archibald Menzies on the platform for the first time in the capacity of 'Conductor'. The minute continues: 'Great praise is deservedly due to our conductor for this marked improvement upon the Society's performances, through the careful training bestowed upon the members at the weekly meetings'. Although the Society, by this time, had a large library of music and was still using the *Athole Collection*, it was agreed to purchase, for the benefit of the playing members, 'Old and authentic copies of Strathspeys and Reels published by composers such as Marshall, MacIntosh, Fraser and Gow'.

The highest honour so far conferred upon the Society came with an invitation from the Incorporated Society of Musicians for a deputation from the Edinburgh Highland Reel and Strathspey Society to attend a conference of musicians from all parts of Scotland, England and Ireland, which took place on 31 December 1895. Twelve members of the Society appeared at this meeting, and their performances of strathspeys and reels before this august assembly gave the utmost satisfaction, duly indicated by letters of praise from the secretary of the Incorporated Society of Musicians.

Although the 1895–96 session was a very successful one for the Society, it also suffered irreparable loss through the deaths of the President, James Stewart Robertson of Edradynate, and the Vice-President, Robert Watson, the Society's Bard.

The newspapers at the time, in mentioning the death of James Stewart Robertson, recorded his fame as lawyer, philanthropist, and politician, but nothing was said of him as a musician. He was certainly deserving of notice for his monumental work the *Athole Collection*, to say nothing of him as the respected President of the Edinburgh Highland Reel and Strathspey Society. James Stewart Robertson was born in 1823 and was a pupil of Duncan McKercher (The Athole Paganini), John McAlpine and William McLeish (The Aberfeldy Paganini).

In 1899 the Mod came to Edinburgh. An Irish Gaelic periodical, *Fainne an Lae*, describes it in these terms:

> This year for the first time, the Highland Gaels invaded 'the finest city on earth' with their musical and literary tournament. – Undoubtedly the finest performance of all was that of the Edinburgh Highland Reel and Strathspey Society. It consisted entirely of men, who stood up in playing – a somewhat unusual thing for a string band. But the effect was marvellous. The reels and strathspeys were played with balance, verve and vigour which simply carried the audience by storm. When shall we have an exposition of our own dance music in Ireland which will rival that performance?

The Society has a medal known as the Paterson Challenge Gold Medal, first competed for on 23 April 1900. The Annual Report of 1 Oct 1900 informs us: 'Through the generous liberality of Charles E. Paterson Esq, Canford Manor, Wimbourne, Dorset, a gold medal was presented by him to the Society for annual competition by the less experienced players, who had made most progress in playing during the session as well as for regular attendance'. Charles Edward Paterson, factor for Sir Robert Menzies and Lord Wimborne, was a wholehearted enthusiast in the matter of reels and strathspeys, and during a lifelong friendship, begun in Perthshire, formed a strong bond of attachment with Archibald Menzies, Conductor of the Orchestra.

On one occasion, he went upon a journey through the North as far as Invergordon in search of players of the traditional style, and he was so disappointed at failing to find a single one that on returning to Edinburgh he asked the then members of the Society to go on a tour through the Highlands in a caravan to try to arouse interest in the music, and offered to give £100 towards this; but instead this medal was gifted by him to encourage the younger members. He was born in 1832 and died in 1905.

Charles Paterson was a pupil of, and greatly admired, Willie Blair, and so it is not surprising to find that this medal is for the playing of 'Reels and Strathspeys in the old Highland or Willie Blair fashion'.

Willie Blair, born in Crathie in 1793, was known to many members of the Society. He was a famous fiddler, composer, teacher, and fiddle maker. In 1848, at Balmoral, he obtained the position as 'the Queen's Fiddler'. He was a pupil of Peter Hardie (1773–1863), who was a pupil of Niel Gow (1727–1807). He died in 1884.

Over the years, many concerts were given in furtherance of the aims of the Society – to promote public interest in our Scottish music. The raising of funds for charitable purposes took precedence over the necessary funding of the running of the Society.

Here are details of some of these concerts:

22 April 1893 – Fifty players appeared on the Music Hall platform with many talented artistes, who all gave their services gratuitously for behoof of the widow and family of the late William McLennan, the celebrated piper and Scottish Dancer.

15 December 1894 – A number of players appeared in the Music Hall in connection with a Bazaar for the Soldiers' Home at Piershill Barracks, Edinburgh. These Barracks were for the various Cavalry Regiments which were stationed in Edinburgh.

2 February 1896 – Following on the death of Robert Watson, Vice-President of the Society, it was decided to make over the free proceeds of the concert in the Music Hall to his Widow and family.

12 December 1896 – twelve first violins, three violas and three double bass players took part in a concert in the Waverley Market for the benefit of Liberton Industrial School.

15 September 1897 – The Highland Mod Society held their Annual Concert in Inverness at which a number of the Society's fiddlers played selections of strathspeys and reels.

16 March 1900 – The Annual Concert held in the Music Hall had upwards of sixty performers on the platform. The minutes record that the Orchestra played 'in a most spirited and expressive manner, there being a strict observance by the performers to the Conductor's baton, and thus securing capital time and tune'. The proceeds from this concert were handed over to *The Scotsman* Shilling Fund for the benefit of the widows and orphans of Scottish soldiers who had fallen in the South African War. Further proceeds were subsequently sent to this Fund.

19 September 1900 – By special request from the Highland Mod Association a large deputation from the Society appeared at the Annual Gathering in the Grand Concert Hall in the Glasgow Exhibition where they gave two performances of strathspeys and reels and played the accompaniments to two choral pieces sung by combined choirs. The Marquis of Graham, President of the Highland Mod Association, wrote to the Society expressing the thanks of the Association for the beautiful music which they contributed throughout the evening.

22 March 1901 – The Annual Concert held in the Music Hall was enjoyed by a crowded audience. The Annual Report covering this concert stated that every part of the hall was filled to excess and that the various items contributed by the Orchestra were received with marked appreciation in a most demonstrative manner. Special mention was made of 'a novel item on the programme for the first time in the history of the Society in having a Lady playing selections on the Great Highland Bagpipes, viz, Miss Campbell of Killin, whose performances were received with the greatest enthusiasm by the large audience. The manner in which she "screwed the pipes" and "gart them skirl" fairly brought down the house'. Again the proceeds were handed over to *The Scotsman* Shilling Fund.

CHAPTER THREE

1901–1914

*I*t is difficult to appreciate the extent of the public interest in Scottish music during the early years of the Society's existence. Music could not be heard unless live entertainments were attended. Now, music pours out in an unending stream from radio and television and is available on cassette and compact disc at the touch of a button.

The years from the institution of the Society in 1881 to 1901 were exciting for the members. Their interest in Scottish music brought about an increase in membership and a new awareness among the Scottish people of the joy of listening to the tunes, particularly the strathspeys and reels composed in earlier centuries.

The membership of the Society built up steadily. Excellent records have been kept, with the result that the progress and variety of the Society's activities can be traced.

By way of illustration, the 22nd Annual Report by the Secretary submitted to the Annual General Meeting held on 5 October 1903 records that at the close of session 1902–03 there was a membership of 302, composed of 58 Life members (many of whom were playing members), 42 Ordinary members and 202 Honorary members. There were 27 meetings for practice in the hall at 3 George IV Bridge at which there was an average attendance of 46. The broad interest shown by such a wide membership must have given great encouragement to the founding members.

The Scotsman commented:

It says much for the perennial interest of Highland dance music that some sixty gentlemen, many of them, probably the majority of them, long past the age of youthful enthusiasm, should meet once a-week throughout the winter to practise these old airs, and should be able to attract so large an attendance of the hearers at a public performance.

Early in 1903 it was suggested that a Golf Club should be started and several members expressed their willingness to join. At the Annual Dinner of the Society held on 1 May 1903, Sir John Gilmour, Bart of Montrave (Honorary President) intimated that he would present a cup for Annual Competition, The Montrave Cup. This cup was first won by Archibald Menzies in 1903. The Graham Medal was presented by William Graham in 1907. The Ferguson Scratch Medal was presented by Colonel W. S. Ferguson in 1908.

The minute books make it quite clear that 'although the valuable "Montrave Cup" presented for competition by Sir John Gilmour, Bart belongs to the Society, the Golf Club is upheld and carried on quite apart from the Society'. The Golf Club of the Society became very popular with the members and went from strength to strength. It had been the means whereby many of the members became acquainted with each other. Up until recent times the above trophies were keenly contested; however, at present the Golf Club receives little attention. Any initiative among the members deserves every encouragement from the Society.

At the Annual General Meeting held on 5 October 1903 Alex S. Calder was elected Secretary and Treasurer, 'moved by Archibald Menzies and seconded by Thomas Gilbert'. A week or so before the Annual General Meeting Alex Calder was walking along Princes Street when he bumped into Archibald Menzies. 'Ah, young Calder, you'll be at the AGM next week, won't you?' 'Certainly', replied Alex Calder. 'Good', said Archibald Menzies. 'You're going to be the new Secretary and Treasurer', and off he went. Alex Calder accepted the job, believing he would be in the post for only a year or so. He held that office for the next fifty years!

The Society's records prior to 1903 are very fine indeed, but thereafter the books not only record the minutes of meetings and financial transactions but include press cuttings, concert tickets, programmes, etc.

On 12 October 1903, it was pointed out that members of the Society had been 'performing at concerts etc. in the city and neighbourhood, and that in the Bills, Advertisements and Programmes of these concerts etc. they were designated as "The Edinburgh Highland Reel and Strathspey Society" and that without the knowledge and consent of the committee, and that on more than one occasion the playing of these members was not of such a character as would reflect credit upon the

Society'. It was further decided that all applications for the assistance of the Society at concerts should be sent to the Secretary and that 'members of this Society, or the promoters of any concerts etc. be not entitled to use the Society's name without authority'.

In the minutes of a committee meeting held on 18 January 1904 it was reported that a Reel and Strathspey Society had been formed in Perth which had asked for copies of the Society's music for their practice meetings. It was agreed that the printers should be instructed to print from the Society's engraved plates such copies as the Perth Society might wish to have.

It soon became evident that the work of the Society in furthering an interest in Scottish music was being noticed. In February 1904 a Mr Sanderson of West Linton requested the assistance of the Society in connection with the publication of a pamphlet, *Queen Victoria's Influence on Scottish Music and Song* and *Burns as a Musician and Song Writer*. It was decided that the papers should be read by members of committee and, if considered suitable, that the Society should subscribe for 100 copies.

The Minute Book lists the names of the members of the Orchestra who played at the Annual Concert in the Music Hall on Friday, 18 March 1904. Under their Conductor, Archibald Menzies, and with William Simpson, the Leader, there was an Orchestra of 62 players:

First Violins	37
Second Violins	9
Violas	5
'Cellos	5
Basses	6

The Scotsman reported: 'The reputation established by the Society in past years was more than maintained on the present occasion by the sixty performers'. *The Oban Times* also reported fully on this concert:

> There was a very large muster of both ladies and gentlemen, and not a few of the gentlemen present wore the Highland garb. The meeting was a most enthusiastic one, thoroughly Celtic in its

arrangements, and in its demonstration of the hearty enjoyment which is characteristic of Highlanders everywhere.

It concluded:

> The committee are to be congratulated on the success of their concert, and it is to be hoped that others may follow from year to year equally successful. Much of the success of the evening was due to the labour of the indefatigable Hon. Secretary of the Society, Mr A. S. Calder, who had charge of the arrangements.

At the very first concert in 1884 a string quartet performed a 'Highland Wreath'. These arrangements were very popular with the players and were performed, by individuals or by small groups, at subsequent concerts. However, it was not until 1904 that a member, Thomas Warwick, moved that the Society should practise a few of the Highland Wreaths during the session. This was seconded by William Laidlaw and was agreed to. 'It was pointed out by Mr Menzies that the practice of Reels and Strathspeys is however the special object of the Society'. Highland Wreaths were arranged by 'Carl Volti', whose real name was Archibald Milligan, born in Glasgow in 1848.

On 13 September 1905, Archibald Menzies reported that he had received a request from the Secretary of the London Gaelic Society to send a band to play at their Annual Concert in the Queen's Hall, London on 2 November. Sixteen members travelled to London and played at this concert where they 'met with a very hearty reception'. A newspaper cutting of the time shows a cartoon of Archibald Menzies, William Robertson and David Irons.

The 24th Annual Report presented at the Annual General Meeting held on 2 October 1905 concludes:

> The Society is now in the 25th year of its existence. Few of the present members realise the great difficulties that the founders had to face. The practice of our National Music had at that time been falling back for some years, and there was every probability that the art of playing the Strathspeys and Reels in the proper style would become lost. The old members were determined however

to revive and popularise our National Music, and their enthusiasm and hard work overcame all obstacles. Let us not forget the credit due to these gentlemen for this good work. The names of Mr Menzies and Mr Simpson must specially be mentioned. During these twenty five years they have stood by the Society and it is largely through their enthusiasm and untiring efforts that the Society is in such a satisfactory position today. Year after year has shown progress and now at its semi-jubilee the Society has a membership of over 300, and what is of equal importance, the aim of the Society has to a very great extent been achieved, for the National Music of Scotland has become and is daily becoming more and more appreciated and popular. The Society is now recognised as a musical force in the city and is favourably known, it may be said, all over Scotland.

A month later, at a committee meeting, it was reported that a letter had been received from the Brechin Reel and Strathspey Society requesting first and second violin, viola, cello and bass parts for four of the Society's sets. It was unanimously agreed to send the music required.

On 23 May 1906, the newspapers reported the death of Thomas Gilbert, who was present at the meeting on 5 April 1881 when the Society was formed. He was born in Knockando, Moray, in 1832 and was a pupil of Peter Milne and James Taylor. The 25th Annual Report presented at the Annual General Meeting held on 1 October 1906 informs us: 'He was a composer of no mean merit and many small compositions bear testimony to his musical skill. Perhaps his best effort in strathspey music was a beautiful strathspey called after Sir John Gilmour, Bart of Montrave, the Honorary President of the Society, which will live long after him'. The strathspey, and accompanying reel, referred to was printed in 1904 and was presented to each member.

The number of applications for the assistance of the Society at concerts and other entertainments was increasing. In the 1905–06 season the members of the Society appeared 30 times. The reason assistance was given in previous years was the reviving and popularising of our national music. The committee had always carefully considered these applications, and in some cases they were refused. The committee felt that it should not appear at any concert during the coming session unless the concert was for a charitable purpose. A few years later the Society were asked what fee they required for a three-day engagement on 30 and 31 December and 1 January: 'The Secretary was instructed to reply that the Society does not accept professional engagements'.

To celebrate the silver jubilee Archibald Menzies, at a previous Annual Dinner, had indicated that the occasion would be suitably commemorated by a 'Niel Gow' festival. The Annual Concert of the Society took place in the Music Hall on 22 March 1907 'In commemoration of the famous Niel Gow, who was born on 22nd March 1727 and died on 17th March 1807'.

Other celebrations were being considered to commemorate the silver jubilee of the Society, and it was agreed to submit two proposals to the members, viz.

I   That a Social Gathering be held to which members may bring their lady friends

II That the next Annual Dinner [i.e. no lady friends] be made the occasion of the celebration.

At a meeting held on 1 April 1907 it was resolved that the Annual Dinner be made the occasion of the celebration.

On 10 February 1908 it was agreed James Scott Skinner should be engaged for the Annual Concert, held on 20 March, for a fee of £5–5/- (£5.25). In the first part of the concert he performed 'Warblings from the Hills' and in the second part 'Scotia's Pastoral Scenes'. James Scott Skinner is first mentioned in the minute books on 18 January 1897 when he was invited to attend an 'entertainment'. The minutes do not record whether or not he attended; however, in *The Metronome, A Musical Monthly*, published in April 1899, we are informed he did attend an Annual Social Meeting of the Society and that 'Mr James Scott Skinner had not forgotten the kindness he received at the hands of the Society when he left for a concert tour in Canada some years ago'.

The reader who is aware of the strathspeys and reels being played at the present time will perhaps wonder why the name of James Scott Skinner, one of the best known composers of Scottish tunes, has not been mentioned until now.

This remarkable man was born in the year 1843. At the time of the institution of the Society in 1881 he was very well known as a performer of the first rank in the art of Scottish fiddling and had just published his first major collection, *The Miller o' Hirn.* Other collections followed. Some of his musical compositions were held in the highest regard. Nevertheless, the music library of the Society contained no selections of the tunes of James Scott Skinner until the latter half of the twentieth century. The reason for this apparent anomaly was twofold. As will be seen from the Objects of the Society, it was formed to play our Scottish dance music in the old style. James Scott Skinner did not write his dance music in that style. Further, while the members of the Society were greatly taken with his best compositions which include *The Miller o' Hirn, The Laird o' Drumblair, Tulchan Lodge, Forbes Morrison,* and played these in their homes, it was felt that most of his melodies were not of the calibre of the music of the 'old' composers. This feeling was by no means confined to the Society. On the death of James Scott Skinner, to quote from the *Aberdeen Journal,* 27 April 1927, under the heading *A Friend's Estimate* by George Riddell, 'one who knew him well, who admired his gifts, and recognised his limitations', we are informed:

> Skinner was a prolific composer of fiddle music. Besides many single sheets, he issued no fewer than five Collections – he admittedly wrote too much, and repeated himself again and again. He was not successful as a composer of song airs or slow airs generally. *Bovaglies's Plaid* may be taken as one of the exceptions. Such tunes as *The Cradle Song, Flower o' the Quern* and *The Duchess Tree* are merely puerile and should never have been printed. It is purely as a Strathspey composer, however, that he has to be considered – on the whole, [he] lacks the charm and spontaneity of Marshall.

It was not until 1953 that the Society began to play Skinner's tunes. It is amusing to report that as late as the 1960s the older members of the Society, when asked to play a Skinner tune, would reply, 'Och, we dinnae want any o' that modern rubbish'.

*   *   *

The Society was still attracting many visitors to the weekly practices, and in the minutes of the 27th Annual General Meeting held on 5 October 1908 it is stated: 'On account of the increasing number of visitors at the practice meetings, and, in particular at the first meeting of each month, it was decided that only friends of members should be admitted and that admission tickets should be provided'.

At a committee meeting held on 23 November 1908 Archibald Menzies reported that a new arrangement of Gaelic Airs entitled *The Thistle of Scotland* had just been issued. He suggested that this new selection should be taken up for practice by the Society, instead of the Highland Wreaths as formerly. This was unanimously agreed to.

The Annual Concert of the Society was held in the Music Hall on Friday, 19 March 1909. As at previous concerts, the hall was crowded in every part and many were unable to gain admission. The Annual Report informs us:

> The Selections of Strathspeys and Reels and Scots and Highland Airs were rendered in excellent style and met with enthusiastic applause from the large audience. The Artistes had each a very hearty reception.

> A feature of the concert was the new Selection of Gaelic Airs, arranged by Mr Alfred Moffat, entitled 'The Thistle of Scotland'. It was considered more difficult than the Highland Wreaths formerly played and grave doubts were freely expressed by many of the Members as to the ability of the Society to play the Selection satisfactorily at the concert. For a time there was undoubtedly some grounds for their fears, but thanks to the encouragement given by Mr Menzies and the indefatigable practice of the Members towards the end of the Season, all difficulties were overcome and the Selection went splendidly and formed one of the most enjoyable items of the excellent programme.

As was the custom at the concerts, bagpipe selections were rendered while the members of the audience were assembling, and during the interval. John Grant played these selections at this concert with great acceptance. A Highland atmosphere was very much present in that 'Valuable assistance was given by several Members and friends in Highland dress who acted as Stewards'. The tickets sold realised £62–5–6 (£62.28) and the payments amounted to £49–6–3 (£49.32), leaving a surplus of £12–19–3 (£12.96).

At the end of the session it was usual to hold an Annual Dinner. On this occasion, Tuesday, 4 May 1909, Colonel W. S. Ferguson, President of the Society, occupied the Chair. The company numbered over 80, which was a record attendance at the Annual Dinner. The usual loyal and patriotic toasts were given and duly responded to. At the commencement of the evening, the Chairman expressed the hope that the speeches would be brief as he wished to have as much music as possible.

The Report on the excellent and enjoyable programme which was submitted amply justified the Chairman's wish that brevity should be the order of the evening so far as the speeches were concerned:

> Strathspeys and Reels were played with great spirit by a large party. A Selection of Scottish Airs by a quintette consisting of Messrs. R. Spowart, A. Johnstone, T. Wilson, W. Kay and Ian C. Menzies was much appreciated. Mr Wm. Simpson played the Strathspey and Reel composed by him entitled 'Ferguson of Pictstonhill' for which he was encored. A pleasing feature of the evening was the singing of the Cap and Gown Quartette. A violin solo was given by Thomas Wilson, a recitation by Mr J. White McLean, songs by Mr Robert Thomson, and bagpipe selections by Mr John Grant.

The 28th Annual Report by the Secretary submitted to the Annual General Meeting held on 4 October 1909 records a small increase in membership to 307. During the previous session, 3 Life, 7 Ordinary and 21 Honorary members were elected to membership. Owing to deaths, resignations, removals from Town, failure to pay subscriptions and other causes, 29 names were removed from the roll of members.

It is recorded in that report that 'A great many applications for the assistance of the Society at concerts and other entertainments in Edinburgh, Glasgow and various other Towns were considered by the committee and the applications were only granted if the concert was of a charitable or otherwise nature'. The minutes of committee meetings give some indication of the great number of requests for assistance at concerts and other functions.

Many applications were considered and parties sent. Others were declined. The minutes state that an application from the Grove Swimming Club for a party to play at their Gala in Dalry Baths on 12 November fell into this category. The Water Music of George Frederic Handel was not in the repertory of the Society's Orchestra!

Within a fortnight, the Wyman Swimming Club and Humane Society were advertising a Swimming Gala in Dalry Baths, stating that there would be 'Selections by members of Scottish Highland Reel and Strathspey' – although no formal application had been submitted. This 'application' was declined.

Throughout the minutes of the Society in the early years there is mention of insufficient double bass players. The double bass is an extremely large, bulky instrument and is relatively fragile. It must have been difficult to transport, other than by horse cab. For this reason, the Society bought a number of double basses for use at practice meetings and at concerts. The 28th Annual Report states that

> there were not sufficient double basses at many of the practices with the result that Mr Menzies was obliged, too frequently, to take a double bass himself. It is hardly fair to expect Mr Menzies to undertake the double duty of Conductor and Double Bass Player and the Society will require to consider whether professional assistance should be called in or whether some of the members should take up the practice of the instrument.

Some of the members did take up the instrument. In particular, Robert Menzies (later Sir Robert Menzies) was complimented on the proficiency he had attained during his first session.

The 28th Annual Report concludes:

> It is gratifying to be able to report the continued prosperity of the Society in every respect. Societies similar to our own, in various Towns with the object of encouraging Scottish Song, Music and Kindred Subjects are now established and doing good work. The credit for this revival of our National Music is undoubtedly, to a very great extent, due to our Society, which has worked so hard and with such success during the past 28 years.

Scottish reel players, about 1850. Back row (left to right): Willie McLeish, Aberfeldy; James McIntosh, Inver; Robert Parry; Jamie Allan, Forfar; Duncan 'Paganini' McKerracher, Dunkeld. Front row: R.B. Stewart, Edinburgh; Archibald Menzies, Edinburgh.

Constitution and Rules

of the

Edinburgh Highland Reel and Strathspey Society

Instituted April 1881.

I Constitution

1. The Society shall be called the Edinburgh Highland Reel and Strathspey Society

2. The object of the Society shall be the Instrumental practice of our National Music, more especially Highland Reels and Strathspeys

3. The Membership of the Society shall consist of Life Members, ordinary Members, (who shall all enter as Amateur players) and honorary members who may not take an interest in the object of the Society (See Rules as to subscriptions)

4. The

First page of the constitution and rules of the Edinburgh Highland Reel and Strathspey Society, 'Instituted April 1881.'

(Above:) ticket for first concert of the Edinburgh Highland Reel and Strathspey Society, 24 March 1884. (Below:) programme of the first concert, in the hall of the Highland and Agricultural Society, 3 George IV Bridge, Edinburgh.

Archibald Menzies (1846–1914), longtime Conductor of the Society's Orchestra.
From *The Metronome*, 1899.

Cartoon of the Annual Concert of the London Gaelic Society in the Queen's Hall, London, 1905. From *The Daily Graphic*.

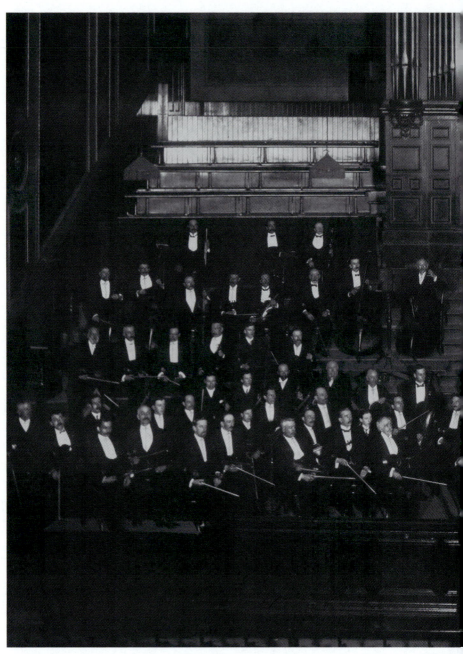

The An

, 1912.

THE

Athole Collection

OF

THE DANCE MUSIC

OF

SCOTLAND.

✠ ✠ ✠ ✠ ✠ ✠ ✠ ✠ ✠

Compiled and Arranged by

James Stewart-Robertson

(EDRADYNATE).

VOL. I.

EDINBURGH:

MACLACHLAN & STEWART.

LONDON:

The title page of The Athole Collection, published in 1883, a collection in two volumes, of reels and strathspeys. Compiled by its President, James Stewart Robertson, who presented the Society with a set.

At the committee meeting held on 6 December 1909, James William Briggs, Violin Maker, 8 Cambridge Street, Glasgow presented a violin of his own make to the value of £20 for Competition by the Members of the Society. Mr Briggs was a well-known and highly regarded maker of violins. At that value, the instrument would be regarded as a fine instrument, much to be desired.

The conditions of the Competition were carefully considered by the committee on 1 March 1910 and it was resolved:

I   That the Competition would be held on the same evening as the Competition for the Paterson Challenge Gold Medal.
II   That the Competition be confined to Members of the Society who had attended at least one-third of the practices during the present session and also assisted at the Annual Concert.
III That the Competitors be out of sight of the Judges and the audience and be known by a number only.
IV   That the Judges be selected from the Society.
V   That the Society present second and third prizes for Competition.
VI   That each Competitor submit the names of three Strathspeys and three Reels from which the Judges would select the Strathspey and Reel to be played, which the Competitor must play three times over.

At the committee meeting held on 19 April 1910, it was reported that James William Briggs, the donor of the violin, had expressed a strong desire that the Judge for the Competition should be a neutral person. The committee thereupon suggested that William C. Honeyman, Cremona Villa, Newport, near Dundee, the well-known authority on violins and violin playing, should be the Judge. He had a wide experience in a similar capacity at many Competitions and had invariably given every satisfaction. Mr Briggs had also thought of Mr Honeyman and had obtained his consent to come.

The Oban Times of Saturday, 30 April 1910 contained a full report on the Annual Competitions for the Paterson Challenge Gold Medal and the Competition for the violin presented by Mr Briggs which took place in the hall, 3 George IV Bridge on Monday, 25 April 1910. The Competitions were held 'before a large and appreciative audience, the accommodation being taxed to the utmost'. Eleven players took part in the Competition for the violin. After a very keen contest, the Judge intimated the playing to be so even as to result in a number of ties. He therefore asked the three highest, who tied for the place of honour, to play a second time, with the following result:

1st Prize, David Henderson
2nd Prize, W. F. Findlay
3rd Prize, Robert R. Millar
4th Prize, A. Greenshields

– the second, third and fourth places being awarded after playing off a tie. 'Mr Honeyman expressed himself as highly pleased with the standard of the Society's playing, and after a selection of strathspeys and reels had been given by the whole of the members, a most enjoyable evening terminated'.

The relative values of 1910 can be compared with those of the present time by reference to the Inventory and Valuation of the Moveable Property of the Society as at 1 September 1910, as engrossed in the Minute Book for that year. A comparison of the values placed on the instruments etc. in that Inventory gives an indication of the more than ordinary attraction of the violin valued at £20 given by James William Briggs for the Competition held in that year. For example, a double bass was valued at £6, cello £1–10/- (£1.50), and a viola ('tenor violin') £1–10/- (£1.50).

At the Annual Dinner of the Society on 3 May 1910, it was related that 'a French University gentleman (an enthusiast in Celtic music)' who had attended one of the Society's concerts, had written to the Conductor in these words:

To you I shall owe one of the great pleasures of my life, the reconstitution before my eyes of that intimate union of music and dance, the tradition and the sense of which the modern nations never had equally with the Greeks. And what I saw was not the fruit of artificial taste such as delights the cosmopolitan audience of modern opera, but a fruit of natural growth which it must have taken centuries to develop to this point of Attic grace. I doubt not that there is music and inspiration in the winds that fan over your heathery hills. I would our musicians would visit the Highlands more.

It is clear that the playing standard of the Orchestra was of some concern to the Conductor and the Committee. Early in October 1910, it was agreed to take up the practice of the Scottish overture *A Nicht wi' Burns* with a view to its being played at the annual concert in the following March. In mid-November, following on the receipt of a request for a party to play at the concert of the Gaelic Society of Edinburgh on 27 January 1911, 'it was resolved not to send a party as it was considered desirable to restrict our public engagements more particularly during the two or three months immediately preceding our own Annual Concert'. *A Nicht wi' Burns* was duly performed at the concert on Friday 17 March 1911.

The concert was reported upon very favourably in *The Scotsman, Edinburgh Evening Dispatch, The Evening News* and *The Oban Times*. The report in *The Evening News* reads:

> There was not a vacant seat in the Music Hall last night when the Edinburgh Highland Reel and Strathspey Society gave their thirtieth annual concert. A pleasing innovation was introduced into one of the selections of strathspeys and reels, 'Corn Riggs' being played as a cornet solo, while a flute and horn lent variety to the melody.

The 'horn' was, in fact, a clarinet. The magazine *The Gentlewoman* also reported on this concert in glowing terms. Regarding Roderick McLeod, the Gaelic tenor, it stated: 'Mr Roderick McLeod's rendering of his Gaelic songs was quite up to his usual high standard. His voice possesses a wonderful softness of tone, as well as being rich and full-toned, and he is heart and soul in sympathy with what he sings'.

On 25 September 1911 it was intimated that Colonel Charles McInroy C.B. of the Burn, Edzell, one of the Honorary Presidents, 'intended to present a challenge medal to the Society and that he left it to the committee to decide what form the competition should take. It was decided to adopt Mr Simpson's suggestion that the medal should be awarded annually to the member who submitted the best Strathspey of his own composition'. By the end of the session this medal had changed into a handsome cup and the conditions of the competition were agreed to:

I   Each competitor must submit an unpublished Strathspey and Reel of his own composition.

II   Each competitor must send his composition to the Secretary, with his nom-de-plume only marked thereon, together with a separate sealed envelope enclosing his name, the nom-de-plume only to be written on the outside of the sealed envelope.

III   The judge should be James Scott Skinner, or some other expert.

IV   The 'McInroy Cup' would be retained by the winner for one year.

V   The Strathspey and Reel securing the first place would be named 'Colonel McInroy, C.B.' and 'The Burn' respectively.

VI   The result of the competition would be intimated at the Annual Dinner.

VII   All the compositions in connection with the cup would be copied and the Society would have the right to publish the Prize composition.

The McInroy Challenge Cup is exceedingly handsome and is much admired. The competition created great interest among the members, and no fewer than twelve competitors came forward. James Scott Skinner judged the competition thus:

	Nom-de-plume	Composer
1st	'Banchory'	William Munro
2nd	'Ettrick Shepherd'	Andrew Greenshields
3rd	'Gowanbrae'	Robert R Millar

This was a good year for William Munro – at the golf he also won the The Montrave Cup and the Graham Medal.

The following year, James Scott Skinner being indisposed by illness and unable to undertake the duty, William C. Honeyman judged the

McInroy Challenge Cup. James Scott Skinner's illness was obviously of some concern to all who knew him. The Society received a letter from Mr MacKenzie of the *Statist*, London, which explained 'that a movement is on foot with the view of obtaining a Government Pension for Mr Scott Skinner in recognition of the work done by him for the good of Scottish Music. It was unanimously resolved that the influence of the Society, as requested, be used to further the object in view'.

On 30 Oct 1911 James Winram, 'the eminent Edinburgh Violinist', gave a lecture on Modern Violin Study:

> There was a large attendance who followed with close attention Mr Winram's very practical exposition of the difficulties of the art of violin playing, particularly the bowing, and the devices by which, to a great extent, it was possible to overcome these difficulties. Mr Winram exemplified his subject by original diagrams and musical illustrations which added interest to a most instructive lecture.

Archibald Menzies heartily thanked James Winram for his able lecture, or 'chat' as he facetiously called it.

On 14 March 1912 Archibald Menzies suggested that the orchestra should be photographed after the concert to be held the following evening.

In 1913 the Annual Concert of the Society was held in the Music Hall on Friday, 4 April. *The Scotsman* of the following day reported the holding of the concert in these words:

> HIGHLAND AND SCOTS MUSIC – That the mission of the Edinburgh Highland Reel and Strathspey Society is not yet spent was evidenced last night when a large and enthusiastic audience filled the Music Hall, in George Street, on the occasion of the Society's thirty-second annual concert. It must have been encouraging to Mr A. Menzies and his Orchestra, and indeed to all lovers of national music, that a programme of Scottish airs should meet with such an appreciative reception. The gentle rhythm of moving feet, that best accompaniment to the Highland airs, and the unstinted applause that followed each contribution, were

ample tributes to the skill of the Orchestra and the ability of Mr Menzies, the conductor.

'SCOTTISH NATIONAL MUSIC – HOW IT IS BEING PRESERVED'
These words head the report of the same concert in *The Northern Scot* of 12 April 1913. The report is full of praise for the efforts of the Society in furthering its aims. The writer of the report was clearly a lover of Scottish music. The following excerpts deserved a wider readership than the newspaper would have enjoyed at that time:

It is thirty-one years since the Edinburgh Highland Reel and Strathspey Society came into existence to practise and keep alive the national airs of Scotland, and how well they have realised their object, and how much they have been appreciated by the public, is shown in unmistakable fashion at their yearly concerts. This annual concert is one of the musical events of the season in Edinburgh, and in its own particular class of music is easily the most popular and the best. Nor are its patrons merely drawn from 'Auld Reekie'. They come from far and near. It is almost like a gathering of the clans, and the tartan is much in evidence.

This year's concert was held last Friday evening in the Music Hall, George Street, Edinburgh, and, as is usual on these occasions, a crowded house, alike of loyal Highlanders and of those who have the disadvantage of birth south of the Grampians, went strongly to prove that our hearts still warm to the airs and melodies of Scotland. There is, of course, deeply implanted in the bosoms of the people a strong love of our national music, and it truly seems as though the Highland Reel and Strathspey Society hold in their possession the key to our bosoms, and can bring that love to surface at pleasure. Much has been written of the deep love of music that vibrates the heart-strings of Scotsmen. It is a tradition that stretches back through history to times immemorial; it is enshrined forever in the deathless song and music of our land, and will endure as long as the snow-capped summits of the mountains that guard our native glens.

And no less pleasing than the music of the violin or pipes to the ear of a Scottish audience are the old songs of Scotland rendered in the 'braid auld Scottish tongue.' These are sweet and acceptable under any circumstances, but they gain immeasurably in their appeal, and strike more forcibly our innermost chords of sentiment, when they are heard far away from the heathery hills and romantic glens of which they speak. They awaken memories of byegone days, and inspire in us the finer feelings of a deep patriotism towards our native Caledonia.

The report continues:

While the concert was a veritable feast of Scottish song and music, it was only natural that the members of the Reel and Strathspey Society should themselves be the principal performers during the evening. They appeared six times, and of their performance too much could scarcely be said. Under the baton of the conductor Mr A. Menzies, they moved in perfect time, tune and spirit. The music was vigorous and full, introducing a touch of light and shade that was pleasing to the ear. Throughout there was a buoyancy of action and an exquisite harmony that made one's blood flow faster, whilst the irresistible lilt of the music set many a foot beating time. What is apt to strike one most forcibly when listening to this Orchestra is that they play together as one man. It is really marvellous to hear fifty first violins, and a total band of over seventy stringed instruments, playing together in perfect time the impetuous rhythm of reels and strathspeys. On listening to such inspiring and exhilarating music many persons in the hall must have had great difficulty in keeping their seats, and one could scarcely feel surprised were the audience to rise and lead off in a schottische or reel o' Tulloch. As it was, the inspiring strains of the fiddles evoked exuberant 'hoochs' from even the most apathetic. . . . So long as these seventy gentlemen are pleased to meet once a week to practise the music of the Highlands, the national music of Scotland can never lose its claim to our affections.

The 32nd Annual Report submitted to the Annual General Meeting held on 6 October 1913 concludes:

It is most satisfactory to be able to report the fact that the Society continues to flourish in every respect. The assets again show an increase, the Membership exceeds 300 and its popularity continues unabated. Societies similar to ours are now in existence all over Scotland, and in England. A new Society has been started in Newtyle, Forfarshire. In far away Johannesburg even, the Caledonian Reel and Strathspey Association has been instituted. Our Society has undoubtedly led the way in this patriotic work of reviving and upholding and creating a love for the National Music of Scotland. It must be gratifying indeed to those pioneers of the movement, our esteemed Conductor, Mr Menzies, and Leader Mr Simpson, as it is to every member, to see such abundant evidence of the success which has attended their indefatigable efforts.

The Members of the Society were deeply shocked to learn of the death of their Conductor, Archibald Menzies, on Thursday, 5 February 1914. The following tributes to his memory are a summary of what was written in the local and national newspapers:

One of the most familiar and popular public men in Edinburgh, and one particularly identified with Highland and Scottish societies, has just passed away in the person of Mr Archibald Menzies, S.S.C. About a fortnight ago he developed a chill brought on by influenza, and towards the end heart failure set in.

Born at Weem, near Aberfeldy, sixty eight years ago, Mr Menzies came early in life to Edinburgh. He began his career as a pupil teacher in Edinburgh, but afterwards entered the profession of the law, and in 1879 was admitted a member of the Society of Solicitors before the Supreme Courts.

A QUEEN'S PRIZE WINNER – Mr Menzies was an enthusiastic Volunteer and one of the most popular men in this connection in the capital. He joined the 'Queen's', 5th. Battalion Royal Scots, in 1863 and was gazetted Lieutenant in 1876. His captaincy came ten years later, and then he became Honorary Major in 1888.

He was one of the crack shots in the Volunteers those days, and, of course, he was well known as the winner of the Queen's Prize at Wimbledon in 1873. His winning of this coveted honour illustrates in a striking degree how great achievements very often depend on comparatively trifling and sometimes accidental details.

Up to almost the last day for leaving he did not intend to compete at Wimbledon, business matters keeping him from entering. A younger brother of his, however, who had entered, was unable to get, and Archie took over his tickets and his entry was transferred.

The winner had a great reception on returning to the Scottish capital. Half Edinburgh seemed to turn out to welcome home the stalwart Highlander who had brought the Queen's Prize to Edinburgh for the first time.

To commemorate the occasion, the following song, which goes to the tune *Highland Laddie'* was written by D. MacKenzie, in July 1873:

The Second Highland Company's
Welcome to
Sergeant Menzies, Queen's Champion

A song, a hearty song, we'll sing,
Resounding rocks the notes will ring,
As every blyth bird on the wing
   Sings 'welcome Britain's champion.'

   All hail our gallant champion,
   Our loyal Highland champion;
   From hill and vale, come clansmen hail
      Young Menzies, Britain's champion.

At Wimbeldon with steady aim,
Honour he won for Scotland's name;
The laureled Highlander we claim
   As ours, Great Britain's champion.

Scotia among her misty braes
Stands buoyant while she sings in praise,
O'er strath and glen in joyous lays,
  Of Menzies, Britain's champion.

Edina, bathed in summer charms,
Sings 'welcome home' with outstretched arms,
And every marksman's bosom warms
  To Menzies, Britain's champion.

Britannia safe may peaceful smile,
Secure within her sea-girt isle,
No foe her shores will e'er defile,
  While breathe her noble champions.

  All hail our gallant champion,
  Our loyal Highland champion;
  From hill and vale, come clansmen hail
    Young Menzies, Britain's champion.

Mr Menzies took a warm interest in Highland Associations. A fluent speaker in Gaelic, he was one of the original members of An Comunn Gaidhealach, and since the days of its inauguration at Oban many years ago, he had rarely missed any of its meetings, and was present at all the local Mods held throughout the country.

Mr Menzies was one of the original members of the Edinburgh Pen and Pencil Club. He was an ardent Freemason. A member of the Lodge of Edinburgh (Mary's Chapel), No.1, he was initiated in 1893, and at one time held the office of substitute Master.

Mr Menzies was a member of the Church of Scotland, having been connected for many years with Greenside Parish Church, in which he held the office of elder.

The affection and respect in which the deceased was held was demonstrated on Monday in no uncertain fashion, by the fact that close on a thousand mourners followed his remains to Newington Cemetery. Many of them were associated with the deceased in the various societies and interests with which he was connected during his busy life in the Scottish capital. At the house in Mentone Terrace, the service was conducted by the Rev. Professor Patrick, D.D., the Rev. John Lamond, Greenside Parish Church, of which Mr Menzies was senior elder, and the Rev. Dr. Rudge Wilson, Wilton, Hawick.

The Edinburgh Highland Reel and Strathspey Society was represented by Mr William Simpson, its veteran leader; its secretary Mr A. S. Calder, and a large number of its playing members.

In the 'concluding remarks' of *A Guide to Bowing* by James Scott Skinner we are informed:

Of course there were natural geniuses, such as the immortals:
Captain Simon Fraser
Niel Gow
[William] Marshall
Airchie Menzies

Of the many tunes Archibald Menzies composed, perhaps the best known is *The Miller of Camserney*.

Following on the death of Archibald Menzies, the Leader, William Simpson, was appointed Interim Conductor with R. R. Miller as Interim Leader. However, William Simpson, on account of illness, was unable to take the rehearsals immediately prior to the concert. Mr E. W. Wakelen, a member of the Society, with experience as a bandmaster, ably took charge of the 1914 Annual Concert which was held on Friday, 20 March. *The Edinburgh Evening Dispatch* reported as follows:

Devotees of our national music owe a big debt to the Edinburgh Highland Reel and Strathspey Society for having so consistently and for so long a period fostered its best traditions. It is not always easy to live up to one's ideals – and seductive are the voices which tempt to the bypaths of ephemeral triumphs – but the Society has never wavered from the set course of presenting good Scots music, well rendered, before its public.

The annual concert of the Society is looked upon as something of an event in the spheres which it influences, and last night's programme submitted to a crowded audience in the Music Hall was peculiarly appropriate, and could hardly have been bettered. It included strathspeys and reels in generous measure, an 'Overture on Scots Airs' and an admirable selection of Highland and other Scots songs by well known vocalists.

Mr Wakelen is a particularly capable conductor, with a valuable and varied experience to draw upon, and under his suave but firm direction the good qualities of an Orchestra of about seventy performers were quickly demonstrated. They handled each item with fine effect and the account they gave of themselves was an excellent and extremely creditable one. Mr R. R. Miller acted as leader in a very competent fashion.

It was not until 11 September 1914 that the appointment of Conductor was considered and it was resolved

to recommend to the Society at the Annual General Meeting to be held on 5th prox. that Mr Ian C. Menzies be elected.

As the son of our late Conductor, and as a Life Member for the past ten years, and one who has played at our Practices and our Annual Concerts, he is well known to us all. No one has a more intimate knowledge of the affairs of the Society. He is a first class musician with a thorough knowledge of our National Music.

CHAPTER FOUR

1914–1920

*T*he first reference to The Great War is in the minutes of a
committee meeting held on Friday, 11 September 1914: 'It was
further agreed to recommend to the General Meeting that the free
proceeds of the next Annual Concert be handed over to the Prince of
Wales National Relief War Fund'. Later, it was agreed by the members
that 'The Surplus from this concert will be devoted towards a Fund for
providing Comforts for the Men of the 9th. Battalion (Highlanders)
Royal Scots on Active Service'. In addition to the war, the members of
the Society must have been very concerned about William Simpson's
health, for on 25 September 1914 'It was agreed that the Society should
pay Mr William Simpson's cab fares to and from the practices during
the coming session'.

Applications for help in the raising of funds for the benefit of members
of the Armed Forces followed in increasing numbers. The first of this
kind was in October 1914 from the Women's Emergency Corps who
were advised that the Society, if the Corps intended to give a concert,
would arrange to send a party to play at it. On 2 November 1914 an
application was received for the assistance of the Society to play at a
Recruiting Concert. This was considered by the committee and it was
felt 'that a pipe or military band would be more appropriate on such an
occasion and it was accordingly decided not to send a party'.

The Edinburgh Gaelic Musical Association arranged a concert to be
given on 11 December 1914 in aid of the War Funds. The Society
agreed to postpone their own special concert in aid of this Fund so that
every assistance could be given to the Gaelic Association by way of
taking part in their concert.

The committee agreed that parties of players should be sent to a
Patriotic Concert in the Usher Hall on 15 January 1915 in aid of a Fund to
provide Comforts for the Highland Regiments. Assistance was also given
at a concert held in Bruntsfield School on 23 January 1915 in connection

with the 9th Battalion of the Royal Scots and to a concert in the Central Hall, Tollcross on 10 February 1915 in aid of the Belgium Relief Funds. The committee also approved an application for a small party to play at a concert for the wounded soldiers at Craigleith Hospital on 29 September 1915 and a concert organised by the Caledonian Pipers' and Dancers' Society of Edinburgh in aid of the Red Cross Fund held in Tynecastle Hall on 15 December 1915. The minutes show ever-increasing applications for assistance at concerts for wounded soldiers or for raising funds for the benefit of soldiers on active service or for the Red Cross.

The Annual Concert took place in the recently opened Usher Hall on Friday, 19 March 1915. The Annual Report states:

> a great audience filled the hall (which has accommodation for about 3000) and many were unable to gain admission. The provision of Stewards for the Usher Hall is no light task and on this occasion the Society had the assistance of 13 paid and highly experienced Stewards for the doors and corridors and 25 non-commissioned officers and men from the 'Dandy Ninth' throughout the Concert Hall all of whom performed their duties in the most efficient manner.

> The sum of £65 from the concert surplus was voted to the men of the 9th Battalion (Highlanders) Royal Scots on active service, which donation was gratefully acknowledged by Major Huie, the Commanding Officer, the Regimental Depot.

The Great War certainly had a huge impact on people's lives but one doubts anyone could have anticipated the following minute dated 11 October 1915:

> The Secretary reported that Mr Stirton, Secretary of the Highland and Agricultural Society of Scotland had 'phoned him that the lavatory would in future be locked and that the members were not to have the use of it. It was remitted to Mr Menzies and the Secretary to call on Mr Stirton and endeavour to arrive at a solution of the difficulty which has arisen.

Presumably a solution was found, as no further mention is made in the minutes.

On 24 February 1916, due to Zeppelin raids which threatened the City, it was reported

> that on account of the Lighting Order which came into operation on 25th inst., it will be impossible to have the usual Practice Meetings in the Hall until the roof-lights there are obscured but that [the Secretary] will arrange that we will have the use of the Board Room on 28th inst. The Secretary was instructed to see Mr John Gardiner, Painter, one of our Playing Members and get him to do whatever is necessary to make the lights conform to the Order. It was agreed the Society would pay the cost.

The work was carried out according to the instructions and 'The Board of Directors of the Highland and Agricultural Society magnanimously paid the account for this work'.

Another small but important dilemma had arisen on account of the war, i.e. the difficulty in obtaining double bass strings. However, it was reported that 'in connection with the great and increasing shortage of double bass strings, Mr T. Eckford Comrie had secured a supply for the Society from Messrs Hawkes and Son, London'.

The 1916 Annual Concert was held on Friday, 17 March. The mobilisation of men into the Forces became noticeable in that two of the performers who appeared on the platform were L/Cpl. J. Bruce, 4th.Btn. (Q.E.R.) The Royal Scots, Tenor and Coy. Sgt.-Maj. Colin MacLeod, Argyll and Sutherland Highlanders, Baritone, both of whom had been wounded in action. The pipers of George Watson's OTC played at the interval. The surplus from this concert was devoted towards the Auxiliary Hospital at 6 Oswald Road, Edinburgh for wounded soldiers, organised by the Scottish Women's First Aid Corps.

The Oban Times, reporting on the 1916 Annual Concert, stated: 'Strathspeys and Reels with their impetuous rhythm undoubtedly lend themselves to individual interpretation, and it is therefore remarkable to find that the orchestra play them as one man'.

A letter of thanks was received from the Scottish Women's First Aid Corps Hospital: 'Please make known the gratitude of the committee of the Scottish Women's First Aid Corps for the very handsome addition to their hospital fund. It came at a most opportune moment, and we desire to offer our most hearty thanks to all concerned.'

At a general meeting on Monday, 20 March 1916, it was resolved that 'on account of the large number of members who are serving with the colours and the probability of more being shortly called up, . . . the Annual Competitions should be abandoned this year'. The golf outings were also abandoned.

Over a period of years, the annual reports made reference to the perfect attendance of William Simpson; for example: 'It is the earnest wish of every member that he may maintain that perfect record for many a year to come. His excellent example may be commended to every member for it is only by regular attendance at the weekly meetings and diligent practice that the high position attained by the Society can be upheld'.

The continuing threat of Zeppelin raids is evidenced in the annual report dated 2 October 1916:

> The perils of the dark and dangerous streets did not in any way affect the enthusiasm of our worthy Leader Mr Simpson who last session had again a perfect attendance record. That he may long maintain it is the earnest wish of every member. The committee hope that every member will emulate his example and that, in spite of the prevailing gloom, an endeavour will be made to attend every practice.

In 1916, the War was far from over. There were many dark days ahead, and the appalling casualties were to continue. The report concludes on an optimistic note:

> The new session opens with the dark War cloud still overhanging but with the assurance that now there is undoubted and cumulative evidence that the dawn of victory is in sight. Long before another session comes round, we earnestly trust Peace may be restored, and that we may have the pleasure and privilege to welcome back amongst us those of our members who have gallantly gone forth and taken part in the World's greatest War.

The surplus from the 1917 Annual Concert was passed to the Association of Highland Societies of Edinburgh, for 'Providing Comforts to Soldiers of Edinburgh Regiments'. Over £20,000, a very large

'Highland Wreaths' were popular arrangements of 'Scotch Airs'. This one was arranged by 'Carl Volti'– real name Archibald Milligan, from Glasgow.

Title page (1904) of the strathspey 'Sir John Gilmour Bart. of Montrave', Honorary
President of the Society, who was present when the society was formed in 1881.

sum in those days, was raised by the very considerable efforts of the Association of Highland Societies of Edinburgh.

At a Social Evening, held on 4 April 1917, the Conductor, Ian C. Menzies, presented to the Secretary, Alex S. Calder, 'who had been called up for service with the Colours, a token of the appreciation of the members of the manner in which he had discharged his duties as Secretary and Treasurer. Mr Menzies referred in most eulogistic terms to Mr Calder's services to the Society during the long connection with it and he presented to him, in the name of the Members, a beautiful inlaid mahogany bureau subscribed for by them'. However, by October, 'the Military Authorities were of the opinion that the Secretary should be allowed to continue in civil life for a further period'.

Over the years, the Inland Revenue, following on legislation by Parliament, have raised taxes and excise duties in many and varied forms. Entertainment Duty Tax was payable in 1918 at a rate based on the price of admission to a concert, theatre or other form of entertainment of the public. In the case of the Society's concert tickets, the charge for the Area and Grand Tier of the Usher Hall was, at this time, 3/- (£0.15). The duty on 3/- was 6d (£0.03). In the case of theatres and cinemas, the duty was paid on the management certifying the attendances of their audiences and the admission charges paid. However, with single events such as the Society's annual concert, each ticket sold had to be stamped with an Entertainment Duty Stamp of the appropriate amount. The adhesive stamps, obtained from any Post Office, were affixed across the perforated part of the ticket so that it was cancelled, to prevent it being re-used, when the stub of the ticket was detached as the ticket was collected at the door of the Hall.

As a gesture to the Members of the Society who paid yearly subscriptions, it was usual at this time to give such of them as wished to attend the Annual Concert, two complimentary tickets. It was made clear to them that their membership did not confer any right to such tickets and that at any time this gesture could be withdrawn. It was with some surprise that the Society learned from the Inland Revenue that Entertainment Duty was payable on the complimentary tickets for the annual concert issued to these members. This claim was rejected 'as the payment of a Member's subscription does not confer the right of admission to the Annual Concert and as the Constitution and Rules of the Society do not specify any such privilege'. Further correspondence followed with Customs and Excise, London. The Board of Inland Revenue offered to waive the Claim for Entertainment Duty Tax for 1916–1917, but took the view that the Tax should be paid in subsequent years. The committee of the Society intimated that they 'cannot accept the responsibility of bringing the Society under liability for 1917–1918 without a Judicial decision'.

On 7 September 1918, the Collector of Customs and Excise served a Complaint on the Secretary, Alexander S. Calder, in which he was charged with having admitted to the concert in the Usher Hall on 15 March 1918, on payment of a lump sum as a subscription and contribution to the Society 24 Ordinary and 131 Honorary members, without furnishing to such members tickets stamped with a stamp denoting that the proper Entertainment Duty had been made in the manner provided by the relevant Finance Act. The Secretary was advised in this Complaint that he was 'liable to an Excise penalty of £50 and in default of payment to imprisonment'.

The Scotsman reported on this prosecution on 30 September, 1918 in these terms:

ENTERTAINMENT TAX TEST CASE – A decision of con-siderable interest in connection with the entertainment tax, and one which, it was stated, would affect a large number of societies, was given in Edinburgh Sheriff Court on Friday, when, at the instance of Thomas Jerome Bennett, Collector of Customs, Edinburgh, Alexander S. Calder, as secretary of the Highland Reel and Strathspey Society, was charged with having admitted to a concert in the Usher Hall on 15 March, on payment of a lump sum as a subscription to the Society, 24 ordinary and 131 honorary mem-bers, without furnishing each of them with a stamp denoting that the entertainment tax had been paid. For the complainer it was contended that the right of admission to the Society's annual concert was part of the consideration which the member received in return for his annual subscription of 5/-. Mr Calder's agent [Ian C. Menzies] maintained that the subscription was entirely intended to defray the expenses of the Society, and that the ticket of admission to the concert was complimentary and not, therefore, subject to the tax. Sheriff Orr sustained the complaint, but as the case was brought as a test one and as the Society had acted perfectly fair and above board, he imposed no penalty. Although it was unfortunate, he said, that a reply to the secretary's letter to the Board of Customs asking for a ruling on the point at issue was not received till after the concert, the fact that inquiry was made showed that the Society had acted in good faith.

At the hearing, the Sheriff agreed with the arguments submitted to him on behalf of the Society and based his decision on the interpretation of the statement printed on the back of the concert programme to the effect that Members receive Complimentary Tickets. He was good enough to indicate that as the committee did not thereby intend to confer upon the members a right to demand tickets, future trouble might be avoided by altering or eliminating the statement. The committee acted in this way in subsequent years.

The carnage of the War continued unabated. It was with the deepest regret that the members learned of the death of five members who were killed in action. Among them was Lt. Arch. R. W. Menzies, Scots Guards, a brother of Ian C. Menzies, the Conductor.

At the practice meeting held on Monday, 11 November 1918,

the Conductor referred in appropriate terms to today's momentous news. The Armistice had been signed at 5 o'clock this morning and hostilities ceased on all fronts at 11.00am. today.

It was agreed that no practice should take place tonight.

The National Anthem was played by the members of the orchestra.

At a committee meeting held on 25 November 1918, 'It was agreed that an Entertainment for the Playing Members should be arranged in celebration of the signing of the Armistice'. This celebration was held on 12 December 1918, at which, we are informed, 'A delightful programme of vocal and instrumental music was submitted and in the course of the evening a short toast list was carried through'.

Even as late as 24 February 1919, the Armed Forces still had a call on enlisted soldiers. The minutes of a committee meeting on that date refer to Regimental Sergeant Major N. J. Affleck, who was home on leave from France, being engaged as organist and accompanist for the forthcoming Annual Concert to be held on Friday, 21 March 1919. At that Concert, the Orchestra, under their Conductor, Ian C. Menzies, consisted of 73 players. All 46 violins played unison in the sets of strathspeys and reels, and as 'First' and 'Seconds' in the Overture *A Skye Dirge* and in the Selection of Scots Airs. *A Skye Dirge* or *McLeod of Dunvegan's Lament* for String Orchestra was composed by Julian H. W. Nesbitt. On 25 November 1915 he wrote to Mr Menzies: 'I herewith send as promised score and single parts of *A Skye Dirge* . . . I trust it will suit your band. If you wish you may have copies made of each part (and the score also if you care) . . . Any copies you may make remain the property of your band and you can play it in memory of your dear father whose kindness I can never forget'. Mr Nesbitt went on to compose many other pieces that have been played by the Society's Orchestra including *Hebridean Lullaby* and *Lament (Cumha)*.

At a committee meeting on 20 August 1919 'It was agreed that a peace celebration Evening should be arranged for the playing members'. This Evening was held at 19 Hill Street, Edinburgh on Thursday, 2 October, 1919. A most interesting and varied programme was enjoyed by a large audience:

> The Trophies and Prizes were presented to the winners of the 'Paterson Challenge Gold Medal' and 'The McInroy Cup' Competitions and the Society's Golf Club Competitions. There was presented to Mr Menzies a handsome mahogany bureau as a small token of the high esteem in which he was held by the playing members.
>
> The members and their friends had the greatest pleasure in welcoming back the following: John Marr, John W. Seatter, John R. Stormont, George Calder, R. Greenfield and Thomas Somers, who had been on active service during the War.

*   *   *

The committee of the Society was meeting almost every Monday evening after the practice meeting to consider applications for assistance for a great variety of concerts and gatherings. To give some examples of such applications, the Society played at The Mod Concert in the Usher Hall, a concert in Craigleith Hospital and another in Chalmers Territorial Church Concert. On 20 October 1919 a concert was held in the Royal Arch Halls for the Edinburgh Field Naturalists and Microscopical Society Conversazione. On 3 November 1919 the Sutherland Association organised a concert in the Usher Hall, 'the object of the concert being to secure funds to initiate a permanent Benevolent Fund to aid necessitous natives or descendants of natives of the County'. Also 'it was agreed to send a party to play at a reception in the Town Hall, Portobello to the men of the 5th Royal Scots' and 'to play at the Rev. Dr. Harry Miller's New Year Entertainments to the Poor'.

On the other hand some applications were refused. For example, the Young Scots Society were arranging a social gathering in Lauriston Hall, at which Lord Haldane was to be the guest of the evening: 'It was resolved not to accede to this request in respect that the meeting was of a political nature'.

The annual report submitted to the Annual General Meeting of 4 October 1920 reported with regret the loss of eleven members by death, including Sir John Gilmour, 'who was one of the Society's Presidents for many years, took a keen interest in the Society and . . . presided on several occasions at the Annual Dinners. He presented to the Society's Golf Club the very handsome and valuable "Montrave Cup"'. This report also covered the Annual Concert held on 12 March 1920. As in previous years, the concert was a huge success, as is evidenced by the newspaper reports. The Orchestra was larger in number, there being 80 players:

> The crowded Usher Hall last night was evidence of the popularity of the reel and strathspey with a Scottish audience, especially when the playing of these is undertaken by a capable combination which can reproduce the lively and vigorous rhythm of this attractive form of Highland music with melodious effectiveness. All the pieces went with a fine swing, and the playing of the band was marked by precision and expressiveness.

William Simpson's long connection with the Society ended with his death on 6 October 1920. His early life and role in the formation of the Society and his book *A Spring on the Fiddle* are mentioned in previous chapters. He was one of the five gentlemen who met on Saturday 26 March 1881 'to consider the advisability of forming a Society in Edinburgh for the upholding and developing the taste for our old national highland strathspey and reel music on the violin'. For the greater part of half a century he had been a member of staff of the Highland and Agricultural Society of Scotland, in charge of their premises at 3 George IV Bridge, Edinburgh. He was always on duty at the Highland Shows which, at that time, were held at various sites throughout Scotland. His first Show was at Kelso in 1872 – a three-day exhibition with a 10/- (£0.50) admission charge on the first day. He was present in an official capacity at the first competition for binders at Bishopbriggs when the 'Hornsby' won the £100 prize. The *Highland Show Daily* reported as follows: 'There was great excitement among the farmers on that occasion, and they looked on with as much astonishment at these new contrivances as did our grandfathers at the advent of the first locomotive into their territory'. Record has it that the farmers, who came in a critical mood to see this new invention, lost their cynical indifference and followed the binder at work in jostling and excited crowds. At the shows in these days there would not have been more than a couple of threshing machines on exhibition.

During each Highland Show, a Concert to Exhibitors and Herdsmen attending was held under the auspices of the Directors. On Wednesday 16 July 1913 the usual concert was given in the concert pavilion. As in previous years, selections of music were played by the Society's Orchestra under the leadership of William Simpson. These were greatly appreciated, as were the contributions of the other artists. At the close of the concert, William Simpson was presented with a silver coffee tray subscribed for by the Exhibitors as a mark of their esteem on the occasion of his last official appearance at the Highland Show, after 42 years' continuous service. Some years before, he was awarded the Highland and Agricultural Society's gold medal for his invention of the indicator of awards used in the adjudicating rings.

When the members of the Orchestra turned up for their weekly practice meeting on 11 October 1920, Ian C. Menzies said:

. . . the members met tonight under the dark cloud of a great and deeply regretted loss. At the Annual General Meeting last Monday evening they unanimously reappointed Mr William Simpson as their Leader. On Wednesday morning he passed away at the ripe age of 76. He said that every member felt very keenly the death of their most highly esteemed friend and leader who had for so many years taken such an active part in advancing the Society to the high position which it now occupies. Mr Menzies read the Minutes of a 'Meeting of Gentlemen desirous of forming an Association for the practice or promotion of Scottish National music more especially Reel and Strathspey playing in the Highland fashion held at 7 St Andrew Square, Edinburgh on Saturday 26th March 1881.' Mr Simpson was the last survivor of the five gentlemen present at that meeting. On 5th April 1881 the first Committee, consisting of three members, was elected and Mr Simpson was one of that number. On 16th February 1885, Mr Simpson was appointed Leader in place of Mr A. C. McIntyre and he continued to hold that office without a break with the greatest acceptance to the Members and to the utmost benefit of the Society itself. It was always a matter of great pride to Mr Simpson to see how each year showed a marked advance in the prosperity and prestige of the Society. He had no equal as recruiter of new members both Playing and Honorary, and even so recent as last Monday evening a letter was read from him proposing the names of four playing members who had been under his tuition. Mr Menzies expressed the deep sympathy of the Members of the Society with Mrs Simpson and his two daughters in their bereavement and the Secretary was instructed to send to Mrs Simpson an excerpt from the Minutes of this meeting.

As a token of respect to the memory of Mr Simpson no Practice took place tonight.

CHAPTER FIVE

1920–1949

*T*he question of who should succeed William Simpson as leader wasn't even discussed. It was obvious: it had to be William Laidlaw.

Requests for assistance continued to come in from many quarters. Most of these were agreed and parties of appropriate size were arranged. The playing of these groups was much appreciated. A few of these requests may be of more interest than others.

Edinburgh Sutherland Association asked for a party of 12 to play at a concert in the Usher Hall on 28 January 1921 in place of James Scott Skinner who was confined to bed and thus unable to appear. With regret this help could not be given as the members were fully engaged the same evening playing at several Burns' Concerts. Again, a request for a party to play at a Carnival in the Waverley Market on 17 February 1921 was not agreed as it had been found from experience that the Waverley Market was entirely unsuitable for stringed instruments.

The erection of war memorials was proceeding all over the country, in cities, towns and villages. At the request of Tranent Town Council, it was agreed to send a party there in aid of Tranent War Memorial.

The surplus from the Annual Concert held in March 1921 was donated to Scottish Blinded Soldiers' and Sailors' Hostel, Newington House, Edinburgh.

The records of the activities of the Society make many references to assistance given at a large number of concerts and other entertainments. Particular reference is made to the International Rotary Convention Concert in the Usher Hall in the 40th Annual Report submitted to the Annual General Meeting held on 3 October 1921. At this gathering, '20 players from the Society gave selections of Strathspeys and Reels and Scots Airs to a large audience which included 1500 Americans who were attending the Convention. The Artists engaged for the concert were of the highest standing in the musical profession in this Country but the items contributed by the Society were possibly the most highly appreciated'.

The following is a paragraph from one of the press reports on this concert:

THE SPELL OF THE REEL – Anyone who thought that our Highland Strathspeys and Reels only gave pleasure to Scotsmen must have had a surprise at the Scottish Concert given for the benefit of overseas Rotarians in the Usher Hall. It is safe to say that never did a Scottish audience let itself go to such an extent as did the American delegates when the Highland Reel and Strathspey Society were at the zenith of their exertions. The 'hoochs' and yells of the visitors could be heard well outside the confines of the hall, and as the music waxed more fast and furious the Yankees threw all convention to the winds and endeavoured, in the limited space available, to give an imitation of the 'Highland Fling' and the 'Eightsome Reel'.

At the practice meeting on 12 December 1921, 'Bailie John Stark addressed the members. He said that on behalf of the Lord Provost he would ask the Society to be good enough to send two parties to play in the Victoria Hall and the Dunedin Assembly Rooms at the Lord Provost's Entertainments for poor children on 27 and 28 [December] when 2000 children [were] to be entertained, 500 in the Victoria Hall and 500 in the Assembly Rooms each day between 12 and 1.30 p.m.' This request was granted and arrangements were made to play at these entertainments. The Lord Provost, Thomas Hutchison, wrote to the Conductor on 30 December, in these terms: 'I shall be much obliged if you will kindly convey my very sincere thanks to the members of your Society who so kindly provided music on the occasion of the Dinners to the poor children on Tuesday and Wednesday of this week. Their efforts contributed very largely to the enjoyment of the proceedings'.

For the first time, the concert programme for the Annual Concert held on 17 March 1922 stated – 100 PERFORMERS. There were six supporting artists: Miss Margaret F. Stewart (Soprano), Miss Margaret Anderson (Contralto), Colin MacLeod (Gaelic Tenor), John H. Mathewson (Baritone), R. C. H. Morrison (Elocutionist) and N. J. Affleck

(Organist and Accompanist). Ian C. Menzies conducted an Orchestra of 95:

First Violins	35
Second Violins	28
Violas	10
'Cellos	10
Basses	9
Cornets	2
Flute	1

The Evening News reported on the concert in the following terms:

> With about 100 performers under him, Mr Ian C. Menzies, the conductor, acquitted himself well. In some of the less familiar strathspeys, with such a large number of violins under his control, a difficult task was presented to the conductor, but his command of this particular class of music resulted in a wholly creditable performance. Specially worthy of comment was the rendering of 'A Hebridean Lullaby'. Here the elusive, haunting and crooning spirit which characterises the old airs of the Western Isles, as distinct from the bolder themes of the reels and strathspeys, received sympathetic treatment. In their selection of Scots airs the orchestra also gave a performance of merit.

During this period, the flood of requests for assistance at concerts and other functions continued. A few of these, picked at random, show the wide variety of the applications.

Social Evening in the Freemasons' Hall, George Street, in connection with the Annual National Conference of the Church of Scotland Young Men's Guild.

Abbeyhill & District Pipe Band Concert in Abbey Church Hall, in aid of band uniforms.

Edinburgh Borderers Rugby Football Dinner in Ferguson & Forrester's Rooms, Princes Street.

Workers' League Concert and Dramatic Entertainment in the Free Gardeners' Hall, Picardy Place.

At the Annual General Meeting, held on 2 October 1922, a letter was read 'with regard to a violin said to have belonged to the late Niel Gow for which the sum of £25 was asked. Mr William Graham stated that he had seen the violin and that in his opinion it was of trifling value. It was agreed not to buy the instrument'.

The 1923 Annual Concert was held on Friday 16 March. Once more, there were 100 performers. The newspaper reports were full of praise for what was regarded as a great attraction. *The Evening Dispatch* stated: 'Although due to commence at eight o'clock, all the seats were occupied ten minutes before that hour, and many members of the public were unable to gain admission'.

It is of interest that the prices of tickets (inclusive of tax) in 1923 were

Area and Grand Tier (reserved), 3/- (£0.15) Evening Dress
　　Optional
Unreserved Area, 1/10 (£0.09)
Upper Tier, 1/3 (£0.06)
Organ Gallery, 8d (£0.03)

Ticket holders for all parts were admitted at 7.15 p.m. On the tickets and on the programmes which were handed out by the local music sellers (no charge for these programmes), was the following: 'N.B. Holders of Tickets for reserved Seats are advised, in order to prevent disappointment, to occupy their seats before 8 P.M. Seats not then occupied may be disposed of to other applicants'.

Such was the demand for tickets during this period that additional tickets were printed for each part of the hall. These were sold at the box office at the hall, being rubber stamped 'ANY VACANT SEAT'. The result was that about the time of commencement, the stewards were extremely busy looking for unoccupied seats for such ticket holders.

At the meeting of the committee on 1 October 1923, an application of an unusual nature was made. This was from the Secretary, Scottish National Fat Stock Club 'for a party from the Society to play during the Club Dinner on 6 December at which His Royal Highness, The Prince of Wales, who is President of the Club is to be present'. The Secretary was instructed to reply that 'their members go out to play at concerts and other entertainments purely as amateurs for the purpose of popularising our National music, that, in this connection, they have on numerous occasions taken part in after-dinner musical programmes but that they have never sent a party to play while a Dinner was in progress as we felt that this was more intended for professional players but that, if it is desired to have a selection of Strathspeys and Reels in the after-Dinner programme, they would be pleased to send a party'. There is no record of any follow up from the Club.

In 1924 the Society sent an invitation to the Glasgow Caledonian Strathspey Society to attend the Annual Concert. At this Annual Concert, held on 21 March 1924, the Orchestra of the Society were photographed.

At the 44th Annual General Meeting, held on 5 October 1925, it was suggested 'that the Society should compile its music into book form with notes on the past and present conductors and leaders'.

The format of the programme for the 1926 Annual Concert, held on Friday 19 March, was the same as it had been for many years. The tickets for the concert were sold by the members and also by the music sellers. As with previous concerts, the Edinburgh newspapers sent their music critics who wrote their reports which appeared in the Saturday editions of their newspapers.

For the first time *The Scotsman* referred to previous concerts in terms which might indicate that its fulsome praise might have been rather overstated. Reporting on the above concert, it reported: 'The Orchestra, a hundred in number, gave a series of groups of strathspeys and reels, with a fine combination of precision, vigour and good tone. The standard of the playing undoubtedly shows a steady improvement. Some years ago there was a certain discrepancy between the number of performers and the volume of tone produced. This, however, has largely, if not wholly disappeared'.

The Evening Dispatch reported as follows: 'With artists who wedded enthusiasm to their ability and an audience that, while critical, was equally appreciative of the fine workmanship of the performers, the annual concert of the Edinburgh Highland Reel and Strathspey Society, held in the Usher Hall, last night, was an unqualified success. Whether it was that the old national music, songs, and recitations were doubly acceptable in these times when imported 'words and Music' are so popular, or that the audience cognisant of the reputation of the Society was aware of the excellent fare to be provided, there was a delightful intimacy created, which made it difficult to conjecture who enjoyed the long programme most – the entertainers or entertained'.

The following is the Report on the Annual Dinner of the Society which was held at Ferguson & Forrester's, 129 Princes Street, on Tuesday, 4 May 1926, at 7.30pm:

The Chair was occupied by Mr J. T. McLaren, President of the Society. There was an attendance of over 100. The Representatives from the Board of Directors of the Highland and Agricultural Society of Scotland were: Mr Thomas Elder of Stevenson, Mr W. C. Hunter of Arngask, Professor Stanfield, and Mr John Stirton, Secretary. The Tir Nam Beann Society was also represented.

The following Toast List was carried through

The Edinburgh Highland and Reel and Strathspey Society
Proposed by Mr Thomas Elder of Stevenson
Reply by Mr Ian C. Menzies

The Directors of the Highland & Agricultural Society of Scotland
Proposed by Mr Thomas Wilson
Reply by Mr W. C. Hunter of Arngask

The Artists
Proposed by Mr John Stirton
Reply by Mr W. T. Dow, Sr., J.P.

The Chairman
Proposed by Mr William Laidlaw

Songs were given by Mr John E. B. Cowper, Mr Alex. Harley, Mr W. S. Tyrie, and Mr George Campbell: Recitations by Mr R. C. H. Morrison: Stories by Professor Stanfield: Violin Solos by Mr Alex. Ross, Winner of the 'Paterson Challenge Gold Medal', and Mr Alex. W. Hood, First Prize winner in the Slow Air Competition: Two Selections of specially harmonised Strathspeys and

Reels by Mr W. T. Dow, Sr., First Violin, and his three sons at second violin, piano, and double bass, along with Mr Ian C. Menzies, 'Cello, and Selections of Strathspeys and Reels by a large party of Society members.

In the course of the evening, the Chairman presented to the Winners the Prizes in the 'Paterson Challenge Gold Medal' Competition, and the Slow Air Competition, and he also presented the 'Montrave Golf Cup' to the winner Mr T. Eckford Comrie.

The sealed envelopes containing the names of the Competitors in the 'McInroy Cup' Competition were opened when it was found that the Trophy had been won by Mr William Munro, the Second Prize by John H. Cranston, and the Third Prize by T. Eckford Comrie. The First and Second Prize-winners were called on to play their Prize Tunes.

Mr N. J. Affleck and Mr W. S. Tyrie acted as Accompanists.

A particularly successful and enjoyable evening was brought to a close with the singing of 'Auld Lang Syne' and the National Anthem.

The 47th Annual Report submitted to the Annual General Meeting of the Society held on 1 October 1928 narrates the story of the removal from 3 George IV Bridge, as follows:

It is with the deepest regret that the committee have had to announce the necessity of removing from 3 George IV Bridge, which has been considered the home of the Society during the forty-seven years of its existence. For that long period the Society has been privileged with the use of the Highland and Agricultural Society's Hall for its business and practice meetings. We fully realise that the kindness of the Highland Society in granting us the use of their hall free of any cost during all these years accounts very largely for the success which has been attained by our Society. The necessity of removal is occasioned solely by the Highland Society having acquired new premises at 8 Eglinton Crescent, Edinburgh, and their intention to sell at an early date their old Headquarters. Unfortunately, the accommodation at the new premises is not suitable for the meetings of this Society and we are thus precluded from taking advantage of the hospitality of the Highland Society.

We take this opportunity of placing on record our deep sense of gratitude to the Directors of the Highland and Agricultural Society for the highly esteemed privilege which they have so long given to our Society.

Our committee gave careful consideration to the question of accommodation for this and future meetings of the Society. The subject presented considerable difficulty in view of the necessity of having a capacious hall for weekly practices during the Winter season and also permanent accommodation for the storage of the Society's instruments, music and other properties. After having inspected several halls the committee were satisfied that the most advantageous arrangement available was the booking of the Pillar Hall in the Synod Hall Buildings, Castle Terrace Edinburgh, for the weekly practices and the renting of an adjacent room in the same building. While the hall has been taken for only the nights throughout the Winter season in which it is required for practices, the room has been rented by the year so that the Society's effects will be safely housed there and the room will be available at all times for the Society's use for committee meetings or otherwise.

The rent of the hall, including payment for the lighting, heating and cleaning, was £32 for the Winter Season. The rent for Room 6 for the year, excluding lighting and heating and local rates, was £16.

As an indication of the monetary value of the privilege which the Society so long enjoyed of meeting free of rent at 3 George IV Bridge, the cost of the accommodation at the Pillar Hall and Room 6 for the first year there amounted to almost £50. The Highland and Agricultural Society then made a grant of £30 to the Society on 6 June 1929 with the indication that this grant would be an annual one. The Directors stated 'that their long connection with our Society is to be maintained and that our efforts in the way of carrying out one of the aims and objects of the Highland and Agricultural Society of Scotland in its early days, viz. "the preservation of the language, poetry and music of the Highlands" was appreciated" '.

At the Annual Dinner of the Society held in the Albyn Rooms, Queen Street, Edinburgh on 2 May 1932 many interesting toasts were proposed, including the Toast of the Society by Mr Robert Park, of Brunstane:

> He said that strathspeys and reels seemed strangely out of place away from the glens and straths of the Highlands, and yet they seemed to flourish mightily in the very heart of the Lowlands. Was it because the exiles here from the Highlands were able easily under the spell of the music to picture the Road to the Isles? They might be ordinary commonplace Edinburgh citizens during the daytime, but at night time on the wings of music they revisited the purple glens and pine-clad mountain slopes. Let them keep up their reels and strathspeys to quicken and enliven the life of the city that bade them a hearty welcome. The existence of the Society was proof of the ineradicable optimism of the human heart, that optimism which refused to be overwhelmed by the flood of depression that had meantime settled over the affairs of humanity. But if they as a nation could capture something of that buoyancy and vigour and high spirit of their reels and strathspeys, then the Society would have done a great service in helping to lighten the darkness and to usher in an era of great prosperity. The reel had no local habitation. Its name suggested free, unconfined, hilarious joy. The strathspey had a home rich in beauty and romance, and as long as the Spey flowed there would be a strath, and there would be a Spey as long as the Grampians endured. He could wish nothing better for the Society than that it would share something of the permanence of that sweet strath among the hills from which it took its name.

The Society made their first radio broadcast on Wednesday, 20 April 1927 when, as suggested by the BBC, a small string Orchestra provided about half-an-hour of 'instrumental music characteristic of the Highlands' in a programme broadcast from the Edinburgh Studio from 7.45 to 9 pm. A donation of £8–8/- (£8.40) was made to the funds of the Society. The following sets were played at this broadcast: *Thomas Gilbert*, Selection of Scots Airs introducing *The Auld Hoose* etc. and *The Marquis of Huntly's Farewell*. The Minute Book records the receipt of this donation and states: 'this sum was used to provide liquid refreshments to the Members at the Annual Dinner on 6 May last'.

The BBC again asked the Society to broadcast on Saturday, 11 January 1930 from 8.30 to 9 pm. A fee of £8–8/- (£8.40) would be paid for behoof of the Society's funds. This engagement was accepted and the sets of strathspeys and reels to be played were decided upon: *Lady Mary Ramsay* and *The Marquis of Huntly's Farewell*.

Further invitations from the BBC were received to broadcast over the following years. These were made on 9 December 1934 when the following sets were played: *Mr Gilbert, Marchioness of Huntly* and *Earl Grey*. On 28 March 1935 three sets were played: *Maids of Islay, Greigs, Newfield Cottage*, along with *No. 6 Highland Wreath*. On 17 January 1936, 13 May 1936, 12 November 1936, and in the following year on 19 February 1937, 9 August 1937 and 9 November 1937 four sets were played: *Newfield Cottage, Miss Jessie Smith, Miss Campbell of Sadell* and *Marchioness of Huntly*. It is recorded that as this last broadcast was on a Monday evening from 7.50 to 8.20 pm., a 'wireless set' was installed in the Pillar Hall that evening so that the members who were not at Broadcasting House would hear the performance. Tape recording machines were unheard of at that time, so a broadcast was a once-only event. There was no opportunity to hear a broadcast programme other than listening to it live. The next broadcasts by the Society were on 19 April 1938 and again on 27 October 1938. The last was on 28 May 1941. For each of these broadcasts, the fee paid by the BBC was £8–8/- (£8.40).

Considerable interest was shown in these broadcasts, whether 'live' or pre-recorded, both by correspondence received from a wide geographical area and by letters to the newspapers. *The Evening Dispatch* of Saturday, 16 May 1936 printed the following letter:

SCOTTISH DANCE MUSIC

To the Editor.

It is gratifying to note that the violin is more and more coming into its own, to hold the prominent place it ought to have in our National music, particularly Highland music.

The bagpipes perhaps may be more suitable for warlike strains and military marches, the violin is the most effective medium for the full and more perfect rendering of that delicacy of expression, and that harmonic manipulation of those fine intricacies which have to be brought out in the successful playing of strathspeys and reels.

A very pleasing instance of this was given by the Edinburgh Highland Reel and Strathspey Society Orchestra in their performance which was broadcast on Wednesday evening, and it would be well if such performances could be repeated at more frequent intervals, since they serve as a stimulus to inspire and encourage efficient reel-playing and other beautiful Scots melodies.

MUSIC LOVER

The Society entered the world of the recording artist on 6 September 1933 when the Conductor and Secretary met Thomas P. Walker, Manager of The Murdoch Trading Company, Glasgow, representing the Beltona Record Company, who requested that the Society should have selections of their music recorded. 'It was suggested that there should be six records i.e. three double sided records or, if time permitted, four double sided records, in case it should be that any of them did not turn out properly. The Company proposed to give a donation of twelve guineas to our music fund'. As a result, four double-sided 78 rpm records were made: Beltona 2096, 2103, 2128 and 2135.

The recording session took place, on 20 March 1934, in the Kintore Rooms, Queen Street, Edinburgh. The process of recording at that time was very different from that used at the present time. The recording was made on a wax disc revolving on a turntable. A needle or stylus, according to the volume and frequencies of the music, cut into the grooves of the wax disc and thereby created the ridges which were subsequently transferred on to the bakelite record. Players who took part in the recordings recalled the difficulty experienced by the producers in keeping the stylus on the wax discs on account of the heavy vibrations of the double basses. The records when released for sale were priced at 2/6p (£0.13) each.

At the time, Beltona said:

> These ancient melodies – how hauntingly beautiful. We like 'The Death of Oscar' best. To hear such records as these explains the popularity of Beltona. Such records carry the soul of Scotland into the homes of her people.

> We daresay that we produce more really authentic Scottish records than all our competitors put together. Good work such as these records exemplify does not just happen, it is the result of thought and careful preparation.

The oldest playing member on these recordings was the leader, William Laidlaw, who joined the Society in 1883, and the youngest was the author, James M. Calder. There is evidence that these gramophone records were used for broadcasting purposes as small amounts were received from Phonographic Performance Limited, London, presumably a precursor of the existing Performing Rights Society and the Mechanical Rights Protection Society.

Reports of the Annual Dinner of the Society held in the Balmoral Restaurant, Princes Street on Tuesday, 2 May 1939 indicate the continuing connection with the Highland and Agricultural Society of Scotland and with the BBC:

> The Society never forgets that its beginning in 1881 is traced to the Highland and Agricultural Society. The close association of the two was evidenced in the presence of about a dozen directors of the 'Highland' at the Chairman's table.

> One of the guests was Mr George Burnett, Public Relations Officer, BBC Edinburgh who proposed the toast of the Society. He said – 'I am delighted to find that in so many country districts

the interest in playing the violin is as strong as ever'. Perhaps, Mr Burnett remarked, there was less boasting about achievement, but that was not a bad thing. It was grand to try to play for one's own amusement. When broadcasting came, many got disgusted with their own efforts. That was the wrong spirit. One could learn a great deal by listening to those more skilled than oneself, but it was only when the heart was vibrating that the strings would respond.

The Society had done a great deal in reviving and popularising the national music of the country. Nowadays, there was so much loose talk about Highland institutions and Gaelic culture. They deplored the distressed conditions of the Highlands, but did they study the causes of that distress? They went to the Mod and told themselves they were going to learn more about Gaelic art, but when the Mod was over, they forgot.

These charges of sentimental laziness cannot be made against the Society. It is a live concern, and has a record of constant progress, and has preserved the traditional style of playing.

During the 1930s, there was a marked decline in the attendances at concerts where classical, Scottish and other music was being performed. This trend could be attributed to the increasing interest in and enjoyment derived from listening to 'the wireless', as a radio was called at that time. The BBC provided full programmes of the highest quality of music, talks, discussion, plays and news. Television as it exists today was a dream of the future. Cinemas increased in number throughout the land, and cinemagoers preferred the more exciting entertainment provided by the colour films being produced. A further element was the great interest in dance bands which played jazz music which was extremely tuneful and encouraged ballroom dancing in the form of foxtrots, quicksteps, waltzes and rumbas.

Many of the Usher Hall concerts, for example by the Reid Orchestra, were very poorly attended. The result of these additional sources of entertainment was that the attendances at the Society's annual concerts dropped. Over many years, the Society had donated the proceeds of the concerts to various worthy causes. The prices of the tickets had been left at pre-1914 levels with the result that the surplus was usually a few pounds.

The 55th Annual Report submitted to the Annual General Meeting held on 5 October 1936 contains this reference to the situation:

> In view of the great difficulty which all concert Promoters have had for some years in securing satisfactory attendances and also bearing in mind the loss of £35–7–10 (£35.39) incurred in connection with our Fifty-Fifth Annual Concert held on 20 March 1936, the committee recently gave careful consideration to a suggestion that a smaller hall be engaged. They decided that, even though there might be another deficit, the Usher Hall should be booked for our next concert and this has been done. The date has been fixed for Friday, 19 March 1937.
>
> The committee were of opinion that, as the Society had taken a leading and highly successful part for over 50 years in reviving and popularising the National Music of Scotland, no step should be taken which would reflect on the prestige of the Society and the success of the National work which it performs. The committee hope that in this they will have the approval and wholehearted support of the Members and that most strenuous efforts will be made to increase the income of the Society in such a way as to avoid future deficits. The two ways in which this can be achieved are by introducing new members and by increasing the sale of Concert Tickets.

From the early days the Society has assisted many other kindred societies in a variety of ways, but perhaps most importantly help with music has been freely given when requested. This assistance ended only when the photocopier appeared. Here is just a summary, covering a decade or so:

Glasgow Caledonian Society – 1927
The Glasgow Society enquired if an arrangement could be made whereby they might have the use of the Society's music plates to have copies of the various sets printed for their members' use at their practice meetings. This was agreed, the Glasgow Society selecting 12 sets. In

addition to 200 first violin parts, 'Copies of the piano, second violin, viola and bass parts of each set were also given to our Glasgow friends'. Their Conductor, Thomas Sinclair Rae, wrote as follows: 'I wish you to convey to your Society our sincere thanks for your great assistance. There are many advantages gained by our Society through your assistance with the music. It has saved a big sum of money at today's prices for engraving. It has saved a great deal of discussion about building up various sets of tunes, and lastly a great many tunes in your sets are quite strange to our members'. Further copies were sent in 1936

Aberdeen Society – 1928

Alex Sim, Aberdeen wrote with regard to the formation there of a Society on lines similar to the Edinburgh Society. He was given all the information he required for instituting the proposed Society. On 2 February 1928, a letter was received from the newly formed Aberdeen Strathspey and Reel Society explaining their difficulties with regard to music for their practice meetings. It was agreed to give that Society every possible assistance, and, in this connection, several complete sets of music were sent. In 1931 a further request was received for copies of the Society's music. The Aberdeen Society expressed their appreciation at being given the use of the music plates for various sets of strathspeys and reels.

Grantown-on-Spey Society – 1928

John J. Davidson, Bank of Scotland House there, a former playing member of the Society, wrote on 26 April, with regard to the formation of a Reel and Strathspey Society on lines similar to the Edinburgh Society. It was agreed to give the proposed new Society every possible assistance. A couple of years later this Society asked for further copies of sets of strathspeys and reels of which copies had already been sent. Their playing strength had increased to such an extent that further music sheets were required. The Society was happy to meet this request. Further copies were again sent in 1935.

Isle of Skye Society – 1929

At the committee meeting held after the weekly practice on 14 October 1929, it was reported that Colonel Kenneth L. Macdonald of Tote, Isle of Skye, who had played at the practice meeting earlier that evening, desired to have some sets of our music for the purpose of instituting a Society in Skye. It was agreed to supply him with the music required.

Crieff Society – 1930
The Crieff Society asked for copies of *Edina* and the parts of *McCrimmon's Lament*. It was agreed to send the music.

Coatbridge Society – 1930
During the session, a deputation from this Society attended one of the practice meetings when they were able to observe the Orchestra at practice. Much valuable guidance was given which was greatly appreciated.

The Land of Burns Caledonian Society – 1930
It is recorded that this Society was formed in December 1929 and that their first concert was held in the Town Hall, Ayr on 26 March 1930. Thereafter the President of this Society wrote, as follows: 'Our Society send your Society their kindest greetings. I cannot think of any Society doing more to keep alive our rich heritage of song. One has only to be present at one of the Strathspey Gatherings to see how these grand old tunes can still put life and mettle in our heels. Again thanking you on behalf of our Society for so kindly letting us have the benefit of your experience through your arranged sets of tunes'.

Glen Society, Glenshee – 1931
Following on correspondence, a supply of the Society's music was sent to this new Society.

Greenock Society – 1932
An application was received from this Society for copies of the Society's music. Four sets consisting of violin and piano parts were sent.

Strathtay Society – 1932
This newly formed Society asked for copies of some of the Society's music sheets. These were sent along with a copy of the Society's constitution and rules for their information.

The Society of Strathspey – 1932
In 1928, the Society were asked by Mr John J. Davidson, Grantown-on-Spey, for assistance in the formation of a new Society. The Society was formed and Mr Davidson, the conductor, reported that the practice of our national music was being taken up extensively in his district. He asked for copies of the Society's music sheets for a further new Society which had been started in Boat of Garten. Further copies were sent in 1937.

Dunkeld Society – 1933
Miss Begg, Ellwood, Birnam, Dunkeld, wrote advising that it had been decided to start a Dunkeld Reel and Strathspey Society. She asked for the assistance of the Society in providing sheets of our music. Violin, piano and bass parts of various sets were sent to her. Further sets were sent in 1934, 1935 and 1936.

Kingussie Society – 1935
This Society asked for copies of three sets of strathspeys and reels with piano copies. These were sent.

Elgin Society – 1936
In October 1936, this newly formed Society asked for copies of the Society's music. Violin, piano and bass parts for four sets of strathspeys and reels were sent.

Tain Society – 1937
There was correspondence with Torquil W. McLeod who, along with others, was arranging for the formation of a Strathspey and Reel Society there. It was agreed to send this new Society, when formed, a supply of sets of strathspeys ands reels.

Society in Toronto – 1937
Mr Hugh A. Ross, Toronto was in correspondence regarding the formation of a Strathspey and Reel Society in Toronto. It was agreed that Mr Ross should be given the information asked for and the music to be played.

Lochee Society – 1938

This Society requested and was sent twenty copies of four sets of the Society's music. In expressing grateful thanks for this music, the President of that Society said: 'We are struggling away with the Society here, but find it a hard task to keep the Players together. There are too many other attractions at present. We have had 25 Players in the Society, but have only 15 Players as yet, this Session'.

Following the outbreak of the Second World War, it was agreed at the Annual General Meeting held on 2 October 1939 that the weekly practices be cancelled in the meantime. It was not until March 1940 that the matter of resuming practices was considered. As the Pillar Hall was not available, it being used for purposes connected with the war effort, it was agreed that accommodation in a hall at No. 1, India Buildings, Victoria Street should be hired for Mondays: 27 May; 3, 10, 17 and 24 June; and 1 July. It is recorded that 39 members attended, the average attendance being 25. The minutes state that 'On account of the "Black-out" and the consequent danger and difficulty of getting about, no practice meetings took place during the Winter months'.

The next Annual Concert would have taken place in March 1940. This concert, which had been an outstanding feature in the musical life of the City, did not take place on account of the prevailing conditions. This was a matter of regret to the members and to the many long-standing and loyal supporters.

During session 1940–41, 19 practice meetings were held from 19 October 1940 to 15 March 1941 on Saturday afternoons commencing at 3pm. These practices were attended by 22 members. The use of Room 9 in the Synod Hall Building was by courtesy of St. Cuthbert's Co-operative Society who charged a nominal rent.

During this period, the orchestra, in a modified form, continued to assist at concerts for deserving causes. In particular, under the auspices of The Association of Highland Societies, a highly successful Scottish Concert was held in the Usher Hall on 23 February 1940. Its object was to provide comforts for Highland Regiments, Soldiers, Sailors, Seamen and Airmen. The Society sent a party of 20 players who took part in a programme supported by Sir Harry Lauder and other prominent artists. On 12 November 1941, the Society sent a party of 15 players to assist at a concert arranged by the same Association held in the Central Hall, Edinburgh to raise funds for the same worthy cause.

At the present time, everyone is aware of the debate on the subject of the European Agricultural Policy which involves subsidies to producers of agricultural products in the many countries of the European Common Market. Again, there has been mention of 'food mountains', of 'wine lakes' and of accumulations of dairy products. Farmers in this country are paid not to grow crops, which is a contradiction of the word 'Farmers'.

How different it was in the war years. Farmers grazed sheep on golf courses – some golf courses were ploughed up and the production of food was a top priority. An Annual Dinner was held on Tuesday, 4 June 1940. *The Scotsman* reporting on this had the heading:

HOME FOOD FRONT
Scottish Agriculture's Part – PLOUGHING FOR VICTORY

Major R. F. Brebner, Chairman of the Directors of the Highland and Agricultural Society of Scotland, in replying to the Toast of that Society said:

> I feel confident about the future part to be played by agriculture in this terrible struggle, and I can assure you that the farmers, landowners and farm workers of Scotland will not be behind hand in doing their job to win victory.

This was in reply to what was said by George W. Ferguson, S.S.C. when proposing that Toast. He spoke of the great need for increased home production:

> Although we had command of the seas, it must be remembered, that every inch of cargo space taken up by the import of food excluded that inch of cargo space for carrying the necessary war material for victory. But war could not be won by force of arms alone. It could only be won by the courage and the soul of the people.

The end of the War brought many demobilised men and women of the Forces back to civilian life. Academic careers which had been interrupted or not even commenced on account of war service were resumed or begun with help from the government and with a warm welcome from the universities and other educational establishments.

At the request of Sir John Fraser, Bart., Principal of the University of Edinburgh, a party from the Society played at a reception for United States and Dominion Soldier Students in the Upper (Playfair) Library of the University, on 13 December 1945. The following letter was received from the Principal:

Dear Mr Menzies,

A much appreciated and valued service merits thanks.

I would assure you that you have such from us in the fullest and most complete degree. This morning I have received innumerable expressions of appreciation of last night's performance. They have come from our Allies and from our own people and the usual comment is – 'How splendid! We have never heard anything like it before.' I am anxious you should know how great is the pleasure which you have afforded and I will be grateful if you will convey to Mr Laidlaw and to each member of the Orchestra our thanks for a most delightful evening.

I am aware of how large a part you have played in the success of the occasion and our gratitude to you is unending.

With kind regards,
I am,
Your very sincerely,
John Fraser

The University held a further reception for the British Dental Association on 4 July 1946 in the same hall. Again a party of players from the Orchestra played selections of strathspeys and reels, Scots airs and country dances. There were also songs from Miss Isobel Kerr, contralto and Mr John Tully, baritone. The whole programme was much appreciated by the gathering of delegates from all over Great Britain. The Secretary of the University wrote: 'May I repeat how grateful we are to you and your players for your kindness in entertaining our guests last Thursday night. The entertainment was a complete success and gave a very fine impression'.

On Monday 15 December 1947 it was reported that 'with regard to the Usher Hall for the Annual Concert, all the Fridays up to the end of March 1948 [have] been booked by the Scottish Orchestra and . . . the only Saturday evening available is 13th March next. It was agreed to book that date for the annual Concert'. Ever since that date, the Society has held its Annual Concert on Saturdays.

The music played at the Annual Concert held on 13 March 1948 followed the pattern of preceding years: four sets of strathspeys and reels together with two selections of Scots airs and *Hebridean Lullaby*. The advertisements for the evening were headed 'Festival Of Instrumental Music, Songs and Country Dances'. *The Scotsman* on Monday, March 15 reported the enlargement of the Orchestra's repertoire: 'A small section of the Orchestra played for two exhibitions of Country Dancing by a team from the Edinburgh Branch of the Scottish Country Dance Society, which included the new dance named in honour of the Duke and Duchess of Edinburgh'. This was the first public performance of the dance. The other dances were *Dundee Reel, Ower Young tae Marry Yet, 51st. Division Reel, Mrs. Stewart's Strathspey* and *Machine without Horses*.

The 67th Annual Dinner was held in the Kintore Rooms on Tuesday, 1 June 1948. In addition to playing members, there was a large attendance of Directors of the Highland and Agricultural Society of Scotland drawn from all parts of Scotland. The Annual Dinner was held on the evening prior to the meeting of the Highland Society, thereby giving the Directors an opportunity to spend an enjoyable musical evening before their meeting on the following morning.

Mr R. Scott Aiton M.C., Legerwood, Earlston, in proposing the toast to the Edinburgh Highland Reel and Strathspey Society, said 'there was an inborn love of music, especially of the fiddle, among the Scots people, and this was not confined to the Highlands. In his own Parish in Berwickshire they would find a fiddle hanging on the wall of every other cottage, and they were all played on. There was a fiddling tradition among the Border hill folk, and there was at least one minister of religion who taught the young shepherds in the district to wield the bow on the 'trembling strings', a practical religion, for surely love of melody and skill in expressing it were akin to worship'.

The records of the Society show that parties from the Orchestra assisted at innumerable concerts and entertainments of a charitable or otherwise deserving nature. Depending on the nature of the event and the size of the place of the entertainment, a party might consist of a few violins with a 'cello and piano or, on bigger occasions, a party of twenty violins with 'cello, bass and piano.

Such occasions were the Saltire Society's two musical evenings in Gladstone's Land on Saturdays 4 and 11 September 1948 commencing at 10pm. These were arranged in connection with the Edinburgh International Festival. Robert Greenfield, deputy leader, was in charge on each occasion when they played before very distinguished audiences.

At the 67th Annual General Meeting held on 4 October 1948, William Laidlaw, who had been a playing member of the Society for 65 years and leader for 28 years, intimated his resignation as leader owing to ill-health. For many years thereafter he continued to take a keen interest in the affairs of the Society. Robert Greenfield succeeded as leader.

At a committee meeting held on 14 March 1949 it is reported that 'With a view to building up a library of Scottish Country Dance Music, it was agreed that Mr John Robertson should be approached to find out if he would arrange a number of Scottish Country Dances specially for the Society and that, if he was prepared to do so, he should be commissioned for this work immediately so that sets might be available for next Session'.

Ian C. Menzies died on 22 July 1949. The Society, in common with others, sustained an irreparable loss:

> He gave his unstinted and talented services wholeheartedly to the Society as a Playing Member for 10 years under his father's baton and as conductor for 35 years. The Society had the advantage of

his intimate knowledge of our Scottish music and his guiding hand and mature judgement in all its affairs during that long period. As a result, the Society has gone from strength to strength so that it now stands as the most famous and influential Society of its kind in Scotland. Mr Menzies' outstanding personality was such that it is difficult to think of the Society without at once associating it with his commanding presence. Mr Menzies' interests were many. He took a prominent part in the life of the agricultural community, serving on many boards where his expert knowledge of agriculture and agricultural law was much sought after. Despite the extent of these other interests the affairs of the Society were ever in his thoughts. He was always ready to do everything in his power to further its aims and objects. As an adjudicator at Musical Festivals his services were in great demand. The Society was represented at his Funeral Service which was held at the Edinburgh Crematorium on the 25 July last. The affection and regard in which he was held by his fellow citizens was demonstrated by the very large number of mourners who attended to pay their last respects to him.

Quoting from *The Scotsman* of 23 July 1949:

Mr Menzies, who was 66 years of age, was the son of Archibald Menzies, S.S.C. As the farmer of a large and very well known holding of Broomhills on the edge of the City of Edinburgh, he had a vast practical experience which was put to good use on the numerous committees and boards on which he served – particularly in the war years.

In 1944 he was awarded the O.B.E. for his services to agriculture.

From *The Oban Times*:

To the Highland community he was best known as conductor of the Edinburgh Reel and Strathspey Society for outside his professional and agricultural work his greatest interest was the traditional music and dances of Scotland. The Reel and Strathspey Society was founded in 1881, and the conductorship during all those 68 years was held by father and son, the father for 33 years and the son for 35. All through the dark and difficult years of the war Mr Menzies valiantly carried on, and it was a great joy to him when the Usher Hall Concerts were resumed the winter before last.

Of the many tunes composed by Archibald Menzies, perhaps the best known is *The Miller of Camserney*.

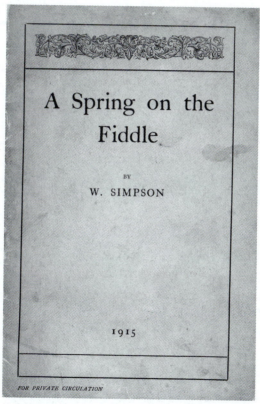

A Spring on the Fiddle, a booklet published in 1915 by William Simpson for private circulation. He was present at the founding of the Society in 1881.

William Simpson

Archibald Menzies

The Society's Orchestra at rehearsal

John Robertson with the Scottish Country Players.

Jean Grant's Strathspey and *Susie's Delight* (reel).

Ian C. Menzies, Conductor of the Society's Orchestra for 35 years, in succession to his father Achabald, who was Conductor for 33 years. Ian Menzies died in 1949.

James M. Calder, who succeeded Ian C. Menzies, retiring in 1991 after 42 years as Conductor. He died in 1999.

In 1976, at the Kelvin Hall, Glasgow, Jim Ferguson led the group which won the *Daily Record* 'Golden Fiddle' competition.

Jim Ferguson, who succeeded James M. Calder in 1991 as conductor.

CHAPTER SIX

1949–1976

*T*he filling of the vacant conductorship of the Society was carefully considered. After discussion it was unanimously resolved to
recommend to the members of the Society that James M. Calder should
be elected Conductor. Both Ian C. Menzies and James M. Calder were
partners in the law firm of Menzies & White W.S. in Rutland Street,
Edinburgh and had been associates over a very long period. Also, the
Calder family had been very much involved over the previous 46 years
and there was very little they did not know about the Society.

The Oban Times, reporting on the Annual General Meeting, informs
us:

> Mr James M. Calder W.S., was appointed conductor of the
> Edinburgh Highland Reel and Strathspey Society at their 68th
> annual meeting. Writing a little after the death of Mr Ian C.
> Menzies, W.S., and speculating on his possible successor, without
> having discussed the matter with any one, I hazarded the guess
> that the new conductor would be Mr Calder. It seemed to me,
> from my knowledge of the personnel of the Society and of Mr
> Calder's abilities as musician and composer, that he was an
> obvious choice.
>
> Mr Calder has all the necessary qualities for the job, and not least,
> an intense love and knowledge of the music in which the Society
> specialises. He has till now been one of the double bass players of
> the orchestra; he has won the special prize for the best original
> composition of a reel and strathspey; he plays the piano, the 'cello,
> and the bagpipes, and on numerous occasions at the annual
> supper of the Society he has shown his versatility by playing
> all sorts of quaint 'musical' instruments, from a saw to an ocarina,
> and has completely mystified the company by his conjuring and
> card tricks [James M. Calder was a member of the Magic Circle].

Reporting on the Annual Concert, held on 11 March 1950, *The Oban Times* stated: 'Mr Calder walked on to take his place on the rostrum. But if there were any doubts as to his ability to carry on a great tradition they were immediately dispelled. Indeed, it seemed to me that while there was spirited rhythm about everything the orchestra played there was also a greater refinement in their tone'.

This concert, for the very first time in the history of the Society, saw the introduction of the piano, played along with the orchestra. 'This innovation proved a marked success.' James M. Calder set about arranging new sets, and on 29 August 1950 'The conductor submitted for the consideration of the Committee certain new music upon which he was working. It was agreed that the selections etc. submitted should be copied and reproduced for the new Session and also that certain further items scored by Mr John Robertson be made available for the orchestra as soon as possible'. The Society is greatly indebted to John Robertson for the use of his orchestrations of country dances, which have been played at many subsequent concerts up to the present day. In particular, a great favourite is *A Scottish Waltz* which was composed specially for the Society.

The 75th Anniversary Concert was held on Saturday 10 March 1956. For the first time a small charge of 6d (£0.03) was made for the programme. The programme notes that

> Except for the War Years the Society's Orchestra with a membership drawn from Edinburgh and District has given an Annual Concert, thereby helping to keep alive and popularise our National Music. The Orchestra is fortunate in its Conductor, James M. Calder WS who, with great enthusiasm and with even greater patience, strives to raise the standard of playing to the highest possible level. In this he is ably assisted by the Leader, John Marr.

> The keenness of the Playing Members, is such that despite the most inclement weather, there is always a very good attendance. New orchestrations are regularly added to the music library, so that there is a great variety of music available for practice.

For the first time also the programme listed the names of the Members of the Orchestra, which totalled 63 as follows:

Violins   46
Violas   2
'Cellos   6
Basses   7
Pianos   2

The artistes who performed at the Concert were West Calder and District Male Choir; Ruth Morrison; Hector MacAndrew (violinist) and George Short.

George Short, a great friend of the Society, first performed at the Annual Concert held on 15 March 1918. Later, he performed in every one of the Society's Annual Concerts from 1934 up to 1962. He provided an organ recital prior to the start of each concert and accompanied the soloists during the concert. Throughout a long musical career (he appeared in a benefit concert for survivors of the *Titanic* in 1912) he was recognised as an accompanist of the finest quality who performed with many of the well-known performers of the day. He had a great interest in Scots and Gaelic music and arranged accompaniments and part songs for Mod Competitions. For a time he was conductor of the Edinburgh Gaelic Choir. He also arranged music for strings. The Society's Orchestra played several of his selections at Annual Concerts and played his Selection of Gaelic Airs at the 1956 Concert.

Dennis Seatter, bass player, remembers the 75th Anniversary Concert:

> The main Guest Artist was Hector MacAndrew, one of the 'Old Style' Master Fiddlers. I remember being very taken with his quiet confidence, his tone contrasts and musical expression. His playing was of a very high standard and he was one player who passed on the Strathspey playing tradition which otherwise might possibly have been lost but for a few players of his calibre and enthusiasm. Looking over the list of the 60 members 'all male' who played on that 75th anniversary on the 10 March 1956, I seem to be the only survivor. I don't know if I should be sad or happy but the memory of a great concert is still there.

At the Annual Concert in 1957, the programme notes that 'The playing strength of the Orchestra prior to the last War was in excess of 100. As a result of that war the membership dropped considerably. Since 1945 there has been a gradual recruitment of good players who have found enjoyment and much of musical interest at the Monday evening practices'.

The programme notes of the 1958 Annual Concert provide background on the music performed by the Orchestra:

> The music played consists in part of Strathspeys and Reels, in sets of 6 tunes, alternating from Strathspey to Reel as found in the earlier Collections. The original settings of these tunes are played.

> In addition to these sets, the Society now has a library of Country Dance music consisting of Strathspeys, Reels and Jigs. To suit the various dances, Strathspey follows Strathspey, Reel follows Reel and likewise with Jigs. The orchestrations are more modern and complex, use being made of 'divisi' string playing and two pianos.

> For this year's Concert, a number of tunes composed by William Marshall have been specially orchestrated in a most attractive way by John Robertson, to whom the Society is greatly indebted. There is also featured in this evening's Concert a Selection of Melodies by J. Scott Skinner arranged by George Short who is always ready to give the Society the benefit of his professional skill.

Whilst the Annual Concerts followed the pattern of proceding years, there are several points of interest in the programmes:

The 1961 concert included a solo performance by Joseph Mathieson, the Orchestra's Leader. He played *Lord John Campbell* (Slow Strathspey), *Forbes Morrison* (Strathspey) and *Millicent's Favourite* (Hornpipe). He gave further solo performances at subsequent concerts which audiences much enjoyed.

On Friday 8 September 1961 players from the Society took part in a ceilidh arranged in collaboration with An Comunn Gaidhealach as part of the Edinburgh International Festival. Also taking part were The Royal Scottish Society Pipers, Edinburgh Gaelic Choir, Lothian Celtic Choir and a number of vocalists and Mod Gold Medallists.

The 1963 Annual Concert started with an organ recital by Lindsay Sinclair. This was the start of a long association between the Society and

Lindsay Sinclair who performed as organist and accompanist at many of the Society's concerts and made a substantial contribution to their success. She studied piano under Mary Moore, taking her LRAM at the age of 19. She has been organist at the Reid Memorial Church, Palmerston Place Church and St Andrew's and St George's Church in Edinburgh and President of the Scottish Federation of Organists. She has undertaken much recital work on piano, organ and harpsichord, working with Scottish Opera and at the Edinburgh International Festival. After being Head of Primary Music at St George's School for Girls, she joined the music staff at Fettes College.

Membership fees had remained unaltered since 1881 at £2–2/- (£2.10) for Life Membership or 5/- (£0.25) per annum. Starting in October 1964, the fees were increased to £3–3/- (£3.15) for Life Membership or 10/- (£0.50) per annum.

The original Constitution of the Society provided that Membership 'shall consist of Life Members, Ordinary Members (who shall all enter as Amateur Players), and Honorary Members who may take an interest in the object of the Society'.

Notwithstanding that there was no exclusion of ladies as members of the orchestra, the few ladies who joined did so as Honorary Members. The question of having lady playing members was mooted from time to time but not supported until 1966, when the Constitution was altered to make clear that lady playing members were eligible to join the Orchestra. As a result the Orchestra that played at the 1967 Annual Concert included ladies for the first time. Three ladies took part in the concert playing the fiddle, viz. Miss D. Bell, Miss J. Wilson and Miss O. Winton. After this the Orchestra never looked back and the number of lady playing members gradually increased and contributed much to the Society. Indeed, it would be hard to imagine how the playing membership could have been sustained without their presence and abilities.

In 1967 after the closure of the Pillar Hall the Monday evening practices were held in the Drummond Hall, Lothian Road Church, Edinburgh. This continued to be used for practices until around 1976/7 when it was converted into a cinema, the Edinburgh Film Guild. Thereafter the move was made to one of the halls in the Highland Church at the top of the Lawnmarket. On the closure of the Highland

Church, around 1978/9, the next move was to St George's West Church, Shandwick Place in which the Monday evening meetings of the Society are currently held.

The 1969 Annual Concert included a performance of *Jean Grant's Strathspey* and *Susie's Delight* (Reel), composed by James M. Calder. Both tunes secured first place for the McInroy Challenge Cup in 1948.

By 1974 the Society's Orchestra for the Annual Concert could boast 71 players. There were also clear signs that the overall standard of fiddle playing was improving, and some players were participating in musical events throughout Scotland. The programme includes the following comments:

> Our Society has matured in recent years and we are proud that such talented young men and women have joined our Orchestra. This evening's concert will show the high standard of fiddle playing. It is no wonder that solo players have taken the top awards in the Prize Lists at Blairgowrie, Banchory, Aberdeen, Kinross, Kirriemuir and at the National Mod at Ayr.

> Joseph Mathieson has been our leader for many years and has delighted successive audiences with his solo performances. The conductor, James Calder, is responsible for many of the orchestral arrangements being played this evening and it is due to his training of the Orchestra that there is such precise playing and excellent musical interpretation.

The important contribution that the Highland Society made to the formation and development of the Edinburgh Highland Reel and Strathspey Society has been described in earlier chapters. The links between both societies had continued for many years with directors of the Highland Society holding office as Presidents and Honorary Presidents of the Edinburgh Highland Reel and Strathspey Society. They frequently attended the Annual Concerts and Annual Dinners and provided support by advertising in the concert programmes.

As time went on, there was less and less contact with the Highland Society, which lost the interest it previously had in encouraging Scottish music and concentrated its attention on its business activities including building a permanent location at Ingliston, near Edinburgh for its Annual Agricultural Show. Prior to this the Show had been held in different towns in Scotland each year. The last director of the Highland Society to be a President of the Edinburgh Highland Reel and Strathspey Society was Mr R. M. Lemmon OBE (1972–75). Since that date formal links between the two societies have ceased.

An interest in and love of fiddling is not restricted entirely to those born in Scotland. Dick Rutter, a longstanding life member of the Society, was born in the South-West of England. Through 'square dancing' he was introduced to fiddle playing and fiddle bands. Having a good musical ear, he was able to pick up tunes quickly, and he taught himself to play the fiddle. For several years he played in a successful fiddle band which he had formed with three friends.

When his employer offered him a permanent position in Edinburgh in 1965, Dick was eager to make the move to Scotland. He was delighted to find that Scotland had a living tradition of fiddle playing with varying styles according to district. He attended Fiddlers' Concerts and competitions and was eventually introduced to Ronnie Watson, a member of the Society, who invited him to join the Edinburgh Highland Reel and Strathspey Society. As he explains:

> My main reason for joining the Society was to learn to read music. By this time I knew most of the tunes that would be played, so I decided to join the second fiddles where you have to play what is written. Ronnie took me under his wing as a competent second fiddle player and I slowly got the hang of reading music. At the time when I joined the orchestra, the conductor, James Calder, used to ask new players to play a tune to the assembly at half time so that we could all assess their playing ability. When my turn came I started sawing away with LONG bows (as prescribed by the conductor) and managed to pull the bow completely off the strings and jam it back again between the strings!

> Using amateur musicians with a wide range of ability, the conductor did his best with surprisingly good results. I am sure

that the standard of playing went up when women were admitted to the orchestra. As time went on I started paying regular visits to some of the older members in the orchestra – John Marr, Joe Mathieson, Willie Hughes, John Thom, Alex Cormack and others.

Dick started with repairing fiddles and then decided to make one for his own use. With great patience and determination he completed his first fiddle in 1972 which played well and then decided to make a viola using local wood that he had seasoned himself. Without a workshop he has continued to make about one instrument a year. Since 1972 he has always played on instruments that he has made himself and has occasionally won traditional fiddle competitions with them. Several members of the Society own a 'Dick Rutter' fiddle.

CHAPTER SEVEN

1976–1991

O n Saturday 31 January 1976, the Society staged a 'Fiddlers' Rally' in the Usher Hall. This was a most successful concert enjoyed by a capacity audience. The Society's Orchestra was augmented by players from other Reel and Strathspey Societies throughout Scotland. The playing of Pipe-Major Iain McLeod along with the fiddlers provided some of the highlights of the evening. The following are the words of welcome to those who attended:

A warm welcome to everyone who has come here to this feast of music. Scottish music has the power to entrance the listener and it will come as no surprise if your pleasure is increased by the enthusiasm and gusto of the players.

Fiddlers' Rallies are becoming increasingly popular and the number of instrumentalists involved in playing our traditional music grows each year. Indeed if our stage was twice its actual size, it could have been comfortably covered tonight.

In addition to the Edinburgh Society's Orchestra, representative players have come from Angus, Ayr and Prestwick, Banchory, Bearsden, the Borders, Dunkeld and District, Elgin, Fife, Glasgow, Inverness, Kilmarnock, North Berwick, Oban and Lorne and Stirling. This suggests that Scottish music with its brightness and spirit has more to offer than other modern forms of musical entertainment.

Stringed instruments, the fiddles, 'cellos and basses are generally held to be the most difficult on which to become proficient. They require the ability to show feeling and emotion coupled with digital dexterity in playing quick notes and runs. The achievement of this makes Scottish music particularly rewarding to play.

Well represented tonight too are the singing voice and the bagpipe, both loved by musical Scots.

'Scottish Records' recorded the concert live before an audience of well over 2,000 people and issued an LP and cassette.

The Fiddlers' Rally was followed a week later by a 'Fiddlers' Concert', also held in the Usher Hall. Again, there was a capacity audience who listened with obvious delight to the playing by the Society's orchestra of a varied programme of Scottish music in all its many forms. An added attraction was the exhibitions of Scottish country dances beautifully performed by a team of dancers in Highland evening dress. The music was played for these dances by a section of the orchestra.

In the 1970s, groups from the Orchestra competed in Fiddle Festivals with great success. One such success was a group led by Jim Ferguson. In 1976, at the Kelvin Hall, they won the coveted *Daily Record* 'Golden Fiddle' competition, with music arranged by James M. Calder.

In 1977, an 'International Gathering of the Clans, Scotland' was arranged. This Gathering consisted of a large number of events held throughout the City of Edinburgh. One of the highlights for those attending was 'The Scottish Fiddlers' Welcome to the Clans', held in the Usher Hall on Saturday 30 April. Over 160 fiddlers took part. The guest artistes were Kirsteen Grant (soprano) and, on bagpipes, Pipe-Major Iain McLeod. To quote the printed programme for the concert:

This evening we have a gathering of over 160 Fiddlers to entertain a Gathering of the Clans. The Edinburgh Highland Reel and Strathspey Society is host to members from the following Societies and Groups: Aberdeen Strathspey & Reel Society; Angus Strathspey & Reel Society; Ayr & Prestwick Strathspey & Reel Society; The Bearsden Fiddlers; The Border Strathspey & Reel Society; Dunkeld and District Strathspey Society; Fife Strathspey & Reel Society; The Highlands Strathspey & Reel Society (Inverness and District); Kilmarnock Caledonian Strathspey & Reel Society; East Lothian Reel and Strathspey Society; and Oban and Lorne Strathspey Society.

The Edinburgh Society was formed in 1881, the main object being 'for the practice of reels and strathspeys on the violin in the old Highland style, in order, if possible, to foster a taste for a class of music so intimately connected with Scotland.' There is no doubt that it has carried out its object for approaching 100 years. Scottish music, so long neglected or looked down upon, has been given its place as one of the main cultural assets of our great country.

Our conductor this evening has directed the music of the Edinburgh Society since 1949. He is a recognised authority who strives for excellence in the interpretation and playing of our National music.

The music for tonight includes many of the finest of our Scottish songs and dances which have been specially arranged for the strings of the Orchestra. Another feature will be the playing of Pipe-Major Iain McLeod with orchestral accompaniment. This will provide the 'new sound' of a 'concerto' for bagpipe and strings. Our Scottish fiddlers are keeping alive the tunes which are our heritage. In the words of Robert Burns:

Hale be your heart, hale be your fiddle
Lang may your elbow jink and diddle
To cheer ye through the weary widdle
O war'ly cares
Till bairns' bairns kindly cuddle
Your auld grey hairs.

This concert was also recorded live by 'Scottish Records' who issued an LP and cassette.

Lord Elgin, the Chairman of the organising committee of the International Gathering of the Clans, contributed a short introduction to the recording. The popularity of Scottish music at this time amongst a wider public may be appreciated from the fact that parts of this concert were recorded and shown later on television.

In connection with this International Gathering of the Clans, a

National Fiddle Competition was organised, with competitors drawn form many parts of Scotland competing for a place in the finals. The three finalists played their selections before adjudicators at a concert on Saturday 7 May 1977 at the close of the Gathering. A second International Gathering of the Clans was held in May 1981, and the Society's Orchestra took part in a Fiddlers' Concert and a Fiddlers' Rally as part of that event.

A Gala Scottish Concert held in the Usher Hall on Saturday 4 February 1978 was the first of the many grand concerts which were organised with the dual aims of sharing with our audiences a taste of the finest achievements of Scottish music, song and dance, and charitable purposes, on this occasion Dr Barnardo's. The proceeds of the evening's entertainment were applied towards their work for mentally and physically handicapped children at Ravelrig, Balerno.

The programme notes gave the audience a taste of what was in store for them:

> Our orchestra will be playing some tunes that are old friends and others whose acquaintance we are sure that you will be delighted to make. All of them have that Scottish 'something' which will surely uplift your hearts and lighten your feet. Our orchestra has been augmented by members of The Border Strathspey and Reel Society.

> Our singers, Patricia MacMahon and Ian Wallace, are superbly able to sing to you of Scotland's colourful heritage, of deeds of love and war and of mountain, glen and sea whose beauties have been an inspiration to the composers of song and are a possession to be treasured for all time.

> In the performances of the Scottish Country Dance Team you will see the graceful accuracy of Scottish dancing and the charm of kilt and plaid.

The Kevock Choir under their Conductor, Alexander Elrick, made a very fine contribution to the varied programme. A cheque for £3,000 was handed over to Dr Barnardo's.

In addition to the 1978 Annual Concert of the Society, there was a Grand Fiddlers' Concert in the Usher Hall on 25 November 1978, organised by the Arthritis and Rheumatism Council for Research (Scotland) in association with the Society. A capacity audience was given the opportunity of listening to some of the best of Scottish music played by the Orchestra. There was the rhythm of the dance music – strathspeys, reels, jigs and the Scottish waltz. There were also the lovely slow airs by the fiddle composers of the eighteenth and nineteenth centuries and the beauty of our Scottish songs played in orchestral selections and as an accompaniment for Kirsteen Grant.

Alasdair Gillies, the Gaelic singer, winner of the Mod Gold Medal when only eighteen, added greatly to the entertainment with his easy manner and warm, relaxed style of singing and presentation. Pipe-Major Iain McLeod played the lighter side of pipe music and the evening was completed by exhibitions of country dances by a team from the Edinburgh Branch of The Royal Scottish Country Dance Society.

The United Nations proclaimed 1979 as 'International Year of the Child', stemming from a belief which is common to us all. Rich or poor, we regard children as our most precious resource. To our children belongs our future. In support of the IYC and to raise funds for that cause, the Society, sponsored by St Cuthbert's Co-operative Society, held a Gala Scottish Concert in the Usher Hall on 1 December 1979. After an introduction by The Right Hon. Lord Wheatley of Shettleston, Lord Justice Clerk, the audience were given a taste of the finest achievements of Scottish music, song and verse.

On 29 November 1980 A Gala Evening with The Fiddlers' Concert was given in the Usher Hall with proceeds in aid of the British Digestive Foundation (For Research into Alimentary Diseases).

1979 was the year in which the people of Scotland rejected devolution in the form that it was offered to them at that time. The programme for the Annual Concert on 10 March 1979 had this in mind when it stated:

Although there was a joining of the Kingdoms in a Parliamentary sense, the people of Scotland maintained their separate identity in a number of ways which included the preservation and development of the music of Scotland. In the 18th and the early part of the 19th century dancing was practised by all classes and the playing of Scottish Dance Music was patronised by Scotland's nobility to whom many of the tunes were dedicated or named after. Balls and assemblies for dancing were frequent and thus did much to encourage the playing and composition of our dance music.

While most of our music is traditional we invite you to listen to the original compositions of Sheila Hart (Ravelrig Selection) and of our conductor (Balvenie Castle).

On Saturday 1 September 1979 the Society's Orchestra gave a Scottish Festival Concert in the Queen's Hall, a new concert hall for Edinburgh, formerly Newington St Leonard's Church. The following year, on 30 August 1980, a concert billed as 'An Evening with the Fiddlers' was given in the Queen's Hall.

On 24 March 1979, the Society's Orchestra, with soprano Kirsteen Grant, contemporary folksinger Iain Mackintosh, fiddler Angus Grant and Pipe-Major Angus MacDonald, gave a concert in the Usher Hall as one of the main attractions of the Edinburgh Folk Festival which extended over the weekend.

The following year, on Saturday 29 March 1980, a similar concert was given. On this occasion, the Edinburgh Fiddlers were joined by members from twelve kindred Societies from the Borders to Inverness. The other artists were Jean Redpath (traditional folksinger), Fraser and Ian Bruce (contemporary folksingers), fiddler Alisdair Fraser, and Pipe-Major Angus MacDonald.

The 4th Edinburgh Folk Festival, held on 27 March 1982, featured the Society's Orchestra and kindred Societies. This Concert opened with Pipe-Major Angus MacDonald playing, from the back of the Usher Hall on to the platform, the *79th's Farewell to Gibraltar* and *Scotland the Brave* with orchestral accompaniment. Jean Redpath and George MacIlwham (flautist) were the other artists. The programme concluded with the audience joining in singing *Loch Lomond, The Northern Lights of Old Aberdeen* and *Westering Home.*

All these concerts required a great deal of ability, dedication and practice, and the Monday evening practices were sessions of great activity leading to tremendous results. So great was the demand that in the period 1979–1981 the Society put on four concerts each year. The players thrived on the challenges, and to help them along it was decided to hold a number of refresher weekend seminars for the Playing Members. These were held in the Queen's Hall, Edinburgh and at Stirling University campus. They were a great success in bringing the players together and advancing their playing technique. Eminent fiddler Ron Gonella and many others gave generously of their professional tuition and advice on these occasions. Ron Gonella appeared several times as an artiste at the Society's concerts.

The finances of the Society were kept in very good shape at this time due to the popularity of the concerts, and there was generally a surplus of income over expenditure from the Annual Concerts in March. The Society decided to fund the refresher courses for the Playing Members from this money and so share some of the surplus with all those who had contributed so much to bring success to the Society.

The concerts attracted more than their traditional support from exiled Highlanders but also support from music lovers from all over Scotland and beyond. It was agreed, in response to the demand, that the Society would give two concerts each year – the Annual Concert and a concert for charity. The Charity Concerts were as successful as the Annual Concerts. They were well supported by the charities themselves and achieved their aim of raising substantial funds to meet important needs.

All these activities required careful organisation, and during this period Ian and Lynn Cameron as Administrator and Organising Secretary of the Society contributed a great deal. Much preparation was required in order that the Society's many large events, such as Charity Concerts and Clan Gatherings, were a success, and the Society owes them a great debt. With their flair, enthusiasm and efficiency they helped to put the Society firmly on the map of Scottish life.

At the Annual Dinner on 17 November 1979 the Society presented a silver salver and crystal whisky decanter to James M. Calder to mark his 30 years as Conductor. The inscription on the salver reads: 'Presented by the members to Mr James M. Calder in recognition of his long and able services as Conductor'.

The Annual Concert to mark 100 years since the foundation of the Society was held in the Usher Hall on 7 March 1981. There were 71 members of the orchestra which included James M. Calder's two sons: Hamish Calder ('cello) and Thomas Calder (piano). The artistes were Linda Ormiston (soprano), Gordon Christie (tenor), Pipe-Major Iain MacLeod and The Royal Scottish Country Dance Society (Edinburgh Branch).

To mark the occasion of its centenary the Society presented a seat in the Usher Hall to the City of Edinburgh District Council. The seat was to the design of the Department of Architecture of the Council and was made in Brazilian mahogany by the Lord Roberts Workshops. At a ceremony earlier on the evening of the Centenary Concert, the seat was accepted by the Lord Provost and was placed in the foyer of the Grand Circle. The memory of the Centenary Annual Concert has been preserved by a number of recordings and photographs. Commemorative ties and scarves were designed by the Society and made to order for the centenary. These proved very popular with the members.

A civic reception at the City Chambers, Edinburgh was given for all playing members to mark the Society's centenary by the Lord Provost, The Rt. Hon. Thomas Morgan. He presented a book entitled *Edinburgh*, with photographs by Douglas Corrance, to the Society's Conductor, James M. Calder, to mark the occasion.

Something new and different was 'A Musical Evening with Regimental Bands and The Edinburgh Fiddlers' in the Usher Hall on 3 December 1983. This concert was to raise funds for the Army Benevolent Fund, the Army's principal charity. It provides help to serving soldiers, old soldiers and their families in real need.

The Military Band was composed of bandsmen from the Scottish Division School of Music and from the 1st Battalion 51st Highland Volunteers (TA). This Band, with the Society's Orchestra on the platform, filled the Organ Gallery of the Hall. It was conducted by Captain D.E Price, the Divisional Director of Music.

The Kevock Choir and Helen McArthur were the singers and Pipe-Major Angus MacDonald played selections of light pipe music. The

Orchestra, in addition to playing our fiddle music, accompanied the piper in certain selections and also played 'Songs for our Audience' with Helen McArthur leading the singing. In addition the Orchestra joined with the Regimental Bands, Pipe-Major Angus MacDonald, Helen McArthur and the Kevock Choir in a performance of 'Ode to Joy'. The concert was recorded live in the Usher Hall by Craighall Studio Production who later issued an LP.

The Society, for well over a century, has carried out much work to help charities, particularly those associated with Scotland. A concert held on 30 November 1985 had as its aim the raising of funds for Soldiers', Sailors' and Airmen's Families Association, which provides a unique service in caring for the families of soldiers, sailors and airmen, also ex-servicemen and dependants. In addition to the Society's Orchestra, the artists were:

The Music Box

consisting of Linda Ormiston and Donald Maxwell, two of the outstanding singers to emerge from Scotland, with their accompanist John Scrimger.

The Kevock Choir

based in Bonnyrigg, which draws its 150 members from all over the Lothians and Fife.

Queen Victoria School

which opened in 1908, and functions as a boarding school for the sons of Scottish servicemen. The boys performed with grace and skill traditional and authentic Highland dancing, accompanied by the school Pipe-Major John M. Mackenzie.

Military Bands

The Band of Her Majesty's Royal Marines;
The Regimental Band of The Argyll and Sutherland Highlanders;
The Band of The Royal Air Force Regiment.

This was a concert of gigantic proportions. The platform was full to overflowing with musicians, every variety of instrumentalists and combinations of these together with singers of great talent. In the long history of the Society, this must have been the grandest concert ever.

Throughout the 1980s the Society continued to perform at least two concerts during each year, one being the Annual Concert and the other a concert in aid of a Charity. Charities that have been supported by the Society in this way are:

1982 – St Andrew's Ambulance Association
1982 – South Atlantic Fund, for all those involved in the Falklands War
1985 – The Western General Hospital Kidney Unit Appeal
1986 – The Multiple Sclerosis Society in Scotland
1987 – Cancer Relief Macmillan Fund
1988 – Kirk of the Greyfriars International Appeal
1989 – Soldiers' Sailors' and Airmen's Families Association and Forces Help Society
1990 – The Viewpoint Trust.

James M. Calder had a long association with the Society. Beginning as a teenage player until retirement in 1991, his commitment was continuous. He joined with Jim Ferguson for his last concert on 9 March 1991 when he retired after 60 years with the Society, including 42 years as Conductor. The first half of the concert was conducted by Jim Ferguson and the second half by James M. Calder. The artistes were Donald Maxwell, Linda Ormiston, Pipe-Major Robert Burns and The Music Box.

The programme for a concert in support of The Royal Blind School on 30 November 1991 includes the following words:

It was to our great regret that, at the recent AGM of the Society, James Calder formally retired as Conductor of the Orchestra, a move which he had been contemplating for some time 'to make way for newer blood' as he put it. James had been our Conductor since 1949 – a magnificent record of 42 years. Beneath his quiet manner lay a deep commitment to the Society and to the furtherance of Scottish fiddle music. We owe him a sincere debt of gratitude for bringing the Society to its 111th and we hope successful year.

At the Annual General Meeting two original watercolours were presented to James M. Calder in recognition of all he had done for the Society. He became an Honorary President of the Society in 1992.

In the field of broadcasting James M. Calder played with the Scottish Country Players and latterly became their Conductor. His interest in Scottish music extended to the bagpipes on which he was an accomplished performer.

His outstanding ability made a great number of new and lesser-known pieces of Scottish music available to the Playing Members, for example modern compositions of John Robertson and George Short. This provided a greater challenge and variety to the Orchestra over the years. The concerts became larger and more elaborate and the Society's orchestra played alongside many of the leading Scottish vocalists and instrumentalists.

James M. Calder died in November 1999 very suddenly. He will long be remembered for his contribution to the quality of playing by the Orchestra and for the many arrangements of Scottish music he made that remain an invaluable resource for the Society.

CHAPTER EIGHT

1991–2001

*F*ollowing the retirement of James M. Calder in 1991, Jim Ferguson was appointed as the Conductor of the Orchestra. Jim Ferguson had been a playing member of the Society since 1967, latterly as Leader of the Orchestra. Originally a student of classical violin, he soon discovered that his great interest lay in playing the wealth of traditional Scots music. He is a talented Scots fiddler and he has joined with Isobel Mieras on the clarsach to perform together as 'Fiddle, Harp and Voice'.

As well as an Annual Concert, the Society has continued to put on concerts in support of charities:

1991 – The Royal Blind School
1992 – Chest, Heart & Stroke, Scotland and British Heart Foundation, Scotland
1993 – St Columba's Hospice
1994 – Marie Curie Cancer Fund.

In 1995, after a gap of several years, the Society's Orchestra staged a Fiddlers' Rally. The Laphroaig Fiddlers' Rally held on 29 July 1995 included 150 fiddlers with representatives from 22 kindred societies.

Jim Ferguson, the conductor, recalls this Rally:

First for many years, and something of an experiment for its timing (mid summer) and for its administration.
So, how did that success come about? Mainly, it was down to three groups of people;
First, our committee, who worked with wholehearted enthusiasm to make sure that the whole day would go like a metronome – which it surely did. Special thanks to our Treasurer, Jim Hogg, our Librarian, Archie Scott, and our Secretary, George Robertson who was instrumental in instigating the whole thing.
Second, our huge audience. For sheer enthusiasm they would have been impossible to beat.

Third, and most important of all, everyone of us who occupied the platform in the Usher Hall. In other words – the musicians. I have to say right away that the orchestra performed way beyond my expectations given the sheer number of players. That the musical standard was so high came down to the prowess of, firstly, our visitors who had surely put in considerable practice before hand and played with such aplomb on the day, and secondly, to our own players who were just brilliant. Every section of the orchestra contributed to what was a great musical evening with superb, rock solid performance. And just in case someone dares to get it in first – no it wasn't perfect, and yes! there were one or two loose rocks. But you can't climb a mountain without dislodging the odd rock, and you certainly scaled the heights that night.

The rally was an outstanding success. The Secretary of the Society, George Robertson, received many phone calls and letters of appreciation. One lady, who had the pleasure and very rare privilege of seeing all four of the Society's conductors, thought this concert was 'superb – the best yet!'

Throughout the 1990s the number of Playing Members has fluctuated between 45 and over 70, with a core membership of around 25 players. Young people come and move on due to the demands of university and career. The talent of the young is of a very high standard due to the importance which schools attach to playing Scottish music. This makes a source of natural ability readily available to the Society. The young from all over Scotland look for opportunities of playing together, especially when away from home, and in Edinburgh this opportunity is given to them by the Society.

The Society has booked the Usher Hall for its concerts since it was built and held its Annual Concerts there continuously since 1915. Due to refurbishment, the extended closure of the Usher Hall, starting in 1997, was a great loss to Edinburgh and meant that the Society had to hold its Annual Concerts in alternative venues such as the Central Hall, Tollcross, and the Queen's Hall, Newington.

The Society continues to help other music societies and organisations. For example, in 1996 the Society gave assistance to Feis Dhun Eideann by donating six fiddles for children, thus encouraging youngsters to practise traditional fiddling. This organisation, on 12 March 1996, wrote to the president of the Society: 'The Feis organisation would like express our sincere appreciation for the goodwill and support you have shown us'.

In recent years the Society has sent music to the Charlotte Symphony Orchestra, North Carolina, and the Roseville String Ensemble, Minnesota, and in summer 2000 the conductor, Jim Ferguson, was invited to the USA to lead instruction, workshops and concerts. This proved to be a great success and is further proof that the object of the Society is still uppermost in the minds of the office bearers.

The Society meets in St George's West Church, Shandwick Place on Monday evenings throughout the winter months. It is open to all who love to practise and keep alive traditional Scottish music, and new players are always welcomed. To maintain a high standard of playing by individual players there are several competitions. Most of these are of long standing and open to all members who compete for honour rather than reward.

The Society continues to have an important role to play in fostering a love and understanding of Scottish music and fiddle playing and looks forward to the future with confidence. To quote from William Simpson's *A Spring on the Fiddle*:

One word I would say to those who are not members is – join, and help to keep alive our grand national music.

The ~~END~~ Beginning

List of Office Bearers

Conductor

1889–1914	Archibald Menzies
1914–1949	Ian C. Menzies
1949–1991	James M. Calder
1991 to date	Jim Ferguson

Leader

1881–1885	A. C. McIntyre
1885–1920	William Simpson
1920–1948	William Laidlaw
1948–1953	Robert Greenfield
1953–1959	John Marr
1959–1990	Joe Mathieson
1990–1991	Jim Ferguson
1991–1997	Bill Chambers
1997–2000	Anna Paton
2000 to date	Kim Beveridge

Secretary and Treasurer

1881–1886	Archibald Menzies
1886–1889	Alex Ormiston
1889–1890	James Chisholm
1890–1891	Andrew MacIntosh
1891–1903	James Chisholm
	(Treasurer, 1892, Andrew MacIntosh)
1903–1953	Alex Calder
1953–1958	Tom Robertson
1958–1966	David Wilkie
	(Treasurer, 1961–1974, Robert McDonald)
1966–1990	Ian and Lilian Cameron
	(Treasurer, 1974–1980, Dorothy Bell/Sharp)
	(Treasurer, 1980–1981, Alex Cormack)
1990–1991	Ian Wallace (Interim Secretary)
1991–1993	Chris Reekie
1993–1995	George Robertson
	(Treasurer, 1993–1999, Jim Hogg)
1995–1996	Cathy Ratcliff
1996–1997	Anna Paton

1997 to date   Nicola Foy
               (Treasurer, 1999 to date, David Service)

President
1881–1896   James Stewart Robertson
1896–1914   Col. W. S. Ferguson
1916–1918   Duncan Stewart
1919–1929   J. T. McLaren
1929–1930   William C. Hunter
1930–1939   John E. B. Cowper
1939–1947   James Paton
1947–1959   Sir Joshua Ross Taylor
1960–1964   J. C. Wallace Mann
1964–1968   A. D. C. Main OBE
1971–1975   R. M. Lemnon OBE
1977–1979   Bill Chambers
1979–1981   Jim Ferguson
1981–1983   John G. Thom
1983–1985   Alex Cormack
1985–1987   Edith Duncan
1987–1989   George Armstrong
1989–1991   Ian Wallace
1991–1993   Jenny Lumsden
1993–1995   Jim Liston
1995–1998   Dennis Seatter
1998 to date   Gordon Reynolds

Honorary President
1896–1899   Robert Cox, M.P., Gorgie, Edinburgh
1899–1920   Sir John Gilmour, Bart., of Montrave
1910–1914   The Rt Hon. The Earl of Stair, Oxenfoord Castle, Dalkeith
1910–1919   Colonel Charles McInroy, C.B., of the Burn, Edzell, Brechin
1915–1961   The Rt Hon. The Earl of Stair, Oxenfoord Castle, Dalkeith
1915–1929   Sir Archibald Buchan-Hepburn, Bart., of Smeaton
1915–1921   Alexander Cross, Esq. of Knockdon/Langbank
1918–1924   Dr Charles Douglas, Esq., D.Sc., C.B., of Auchlochan
1918–1930   Sir David Wilson, Bart., of Carbeth
1920–1923   David Ferrie, Esq., of Parbroath, Cupar
1924–1925   Sir Hugh Shaw Stewart, Bart., of Greenock and Blackhall
1924–1930   The Rt Hon. Lord Forteviot
1924–1930   Sir Kenneth Mackenzie, Bart., of Gairloch
1929–1948   J.T. McLaren., Stirling
1930–1945   Col. F. J. Curruthers, of Dormont
1930–1937   Thomas Elder, Esq., of Stevenson
1930–1941   William C. Hunter, Esq., of Arngask
1933–1948   Sir Iain Colquhoun, Bart., of Luss

1938–1947   Sir Joshua P. Ross-Taylor, Mungoswalls, Duns
1938–1947   Alexander Murdoch, Esq., East Hillside
1945–1952   Maj. R. F. Brebner C.B.E., The Leochold, Dalmeny
1949–1968   The Rt Hon. The Earl of Elgin and Kincardine
1949–1967   Sir Robert Menzies, Heather Wells, Lightwater, Surrey
1949–1970   J. R. Lumsden, Esq., C.B.E., of Arden, Alexandria
1964–1977   J. C. Wallace Mann., C.B.E., Carrington Barns
1968–1978   Miss A. C. Menzies, Edinburgh
1978 to date The Rt Hon. The Earl of Elgin and Kincardine
1991–1999   James M. Calder, W.S., Edinburgh

APPENDIX B

Winners of Competitions

Paterson Challenge Gold Medal

For playing members of the Society under 30 years of age.
Strathspey and Reel

1900	Matthew Keddie
1901	John Ritchie
1902	Matthew Keddie
1903	William Duncan
1904	Robert Spowart
1905	Archibald Adamson
1906	James Sheridan
1907	William Munro
1908	A. McGregor
1909	Thomas Wilson
1910	Robert Cooper
1911	W. B. Henderson
1912	William Millar
1913	Alexander Cochrane
1914	Robert Greenfield
1915	W. R. E. Thom
1916–1918	No competition on account of the war
1919	Alexander Edward
1920	John Marr
1921	Andrew Wilson
1922	Archibald J. Baxter
1923	Alexander W. Hood
1924	John H. Cranston
1925	Robert Hossack
1926	Alexander Ross
1927	James Scobie
1928	John Burnett
1929	Alexander Wilson
1930	Thomas Falconer
1931	Thomas Falconer
1932	Walter Rutherford
1933	David Hall
1934	Alfred Crombie
1935	Thomas Marshall

1936	George E. M. White
1937	James B. Pringle
1938	David T. Hardie
1939	William McIntosh, Jnr
1940–1946	No competition on account of the war
1947	Joseph Mathieson
1948	Malcolm Macdonald
1949	William Murray
1950	James Wight
1951	Andrew Kinghorn
1952	William C. Ritchie
1953	Thomas King
1954–1993	No Record
1994	Anna McMillin
1995	No Entries
1996	David Anderson
1997	No Entries
1998	Anna Forbes
1999	Anna Forbes
2000	Kim Beveridge
2001	Nicola Cruickshank

McInroy Cup

For best original composition for Strathspey and Reel in the old style.

1912	William Munro
1913	Robert Spowart
1914	Andrew Greenshields
1915	Robert Spowart
1916–1918	No competition on account of the war
1919	William Munro
1920	William Munro
1921	T. Eckford Comrie
1922	William Munro
1923	John Craig
1924	John Craig
1925	William Munro
1926	William Munro
1927	William Munro
1928	Andrew Greenshields
1929	Andrew Greenshields
1930	William Munro
1931	T. Eckford Comrie
1932	William Laidlaw
1933	T. Eckford Comrie
1934	William Laidlaw

1935	Mrs E. R. Robins
1936	William Laidlaw
1937	William Laidlaw
1938	Mrs E. R. Robins
1939	William Laidlaw
1940	R. B. M. Blackstock
1941–1946	No competition on account of the war
1947	James M. Calder
1948	James M. Calder
1949	John G. Thom
1950	John G. Thom
1951	R.B.M. Blackstone
1952	Captain Andrew Smith
1953	John G. Thom
1954	Captain Andrew Smith
1955	Captain Andrew Smith
1956	John G. Thom
1957	Stephan Hastie
1958	Captain Andrew Smith
1959	Captain Andrew Smith
1960	Stephan Hastie
1961	Stephan Hastie
1962	Angus R. MacIntosh
1963	Captain Andrew Smith
1964	Captain Andrew Smith
1965	Captain Andrew Smith
1966	R. Watson
1967	R. Watson
1968	J. Ferguson
1969	Sheila Hart
1970	W. MacDonald Hughes
1971	Sheila Hart
1972	John G. Thom
1973	Sheila Hart
1974	Sheila Hart
1975	Sheila Hart
1976	R. Watson
1977	Sheila Hart
1978	Sheila Hart
1979	Sheila Hart
1980	No Entries
1981	No Entries
1982	Sheila Hart
1983	No Entries
1984	Marie Fielding
1985	Douglas Anderson
1986	Douglas Anderson

1987	George H. Armstrong
1988	No Entries
1989	No Entries
1990	No Entries
1991	Alex Lawson
1992	Alex Lawson
1993	No Entries
1994	Alex Lawson
1995	Archie Scott
1996	James M. Calder
1997	Archie Scott
1998	Alex Lawson
1999	Archie Scott
2000	Joyce Brockie
2001	No Entries

Slow Air Competition.
Later known as the **Thomas Eckford Comrie Memorial Quaich**

1922	John Marr
1923	T. Eckford Comrie
1924	Andrew McLean
1925	Robert Hossack
1926	Alexander W. Hood
1927	John Burnett
1928	John Burnett
1929	Alexander Wilson
1930	Thomas Falconer
1931	Alfred Crombie
1932	James Tucker
1933	William Elliot
1934	Thomas Marshall
1935	George E. M. White
1936	David Hall
1937	R. B. M. Blackstock
1938	George E. M. White
1939	William McIntosh, Jnr
1940–1946	No competition on account of the war
1947	George E. M. White
1948	George E. M. White
1949	William Murray
1950	Joseph Mathieson
1951	Adam Darling
1952	Malcolm Macdonald
1953	James Wight
1954–1985	No Record

1986	Joanne Munro
1987–1992	No Record
1993	Celia McIntyre
1994	Willie Martin
1995	Douglas Anderson
1996	Alex Lawson
1997	Alex Lawson
1998	Archie Scott
1999	Alex Lawson
2000	Kim Beveridge
2001	George Robertson

Cleghorn Challenge Cup
For playing members of the Society under 30 years of age.
Slow Scots Air

1950	James Wight
1951	Andrew Kinghorn
1952	James Wight
1953	Thomas King
1954–1974	No Record
1975	J. Neil
1976	B. B. Birse
1977	J. Neil
1978	D. Stewart
1979	D. Stewart
1990	Joanne Slater
1991	David Anderson
1992	Dawn Fraser
1993	Annabel Gillan
1994	Anna McMillin
1995	Sally McIntosh
1996	David Anderson
1997	No Entries
1998	Anna Forbes
1999	Bobby Pendreigh
2000	Kim Beveridge
2001	Kim Beveridge

J. Murdoch Henderson Silver Challenge Cup
Confined to the compositions of the late John Murdoch Henderson

| 1974 | Yla Steven |
| 1975 | Dick Rutter |

1976	B. B. Birse
1977	A. Little
1978	Jim Ferguson
1979	D. Stewart
1980–1982	No Record
1983	Anne Cannon
1984–1987	No Record
1988	George Armstrong
1989	No Entries
1990	Willie Martin
1991	Sheila Hart
1992	Alex Lawson
1993	No Entries
1994	David Anderson
1995	Anna McMillin
1996	Archie Scott
1997	No Entries
1998	Jim Hogg
1999	Dick Rutter
2000	No Entries
2001	No Entries

Maxwell Chalmers Gillespie Quaich

For Group Competition.
Slow Air, March, Strathspey and Reel

	Group Leader
1979	Joe Mathieson
1980	Douglas Anderson
1981	No Entries
1982	Joe Mathieson
1983	Joe Mathieson
1984	Douglas Anderson
1985	Douglas Anderson
1986	Douglas Anderson
1987	No Entries
1988	Douglas Anderson
1989	No Entries
1990	Douglas Anderson
1991	Douglas Anderson
1992	Dick Rutter
1993	Douglas Anderson
1994	David Anderson
1995	Douglas Anderson
1996	Dick Rutter

1997	Dick Rutter
1998	Alex Lawson
1999	Kim Beveridge
2000	Dick Rutter

Joe Mathieson Bowl
March, Strathspey and Reel

1991	Dick Rutter
1992	Celia McIntyre
1993	George Robertson
1994	David Anderson
1995	Anna McMillin
1996	David Anderson
1997	Dick Rutter
1998	Rachael Dutton
1999	Alex Lawson
2000	Nicola Cruickshank
2001	George Robertson

Recordings

The Society entered the world of the recording artist in 1933 when the Conductor and Secretary met a representative of the Beltona Record Company who proposed that the Society should have selections of their music recorded. This resulted in four 78 rpm records being recorded in 1934:

Beltona 2096
Bas Osgar – The Marchioness of Huntly Strathspey – Speed the Plough Reel.
The Marquis of Huntly's Farewell – The Lea Rig – Perthshire Volunteers – Mason's Apron.

Beltona 2128
The Lass o' Patie's Mill – The Duchess' Slipper – Loch Earn.
Stumpie – Duns Dings A' – The Miller o' Drone – The De'il Amang the Tailors.

Beltona 2103
Lassie Look Before Ye – Glen Ogle – Lord Lyndoch – The Moray Club.
Lady Mary Ramsay – Rachel Rae – Marquis of Huntly's Highland Fling – Leslie.

Beltona 2135
The Auld Scotch Sangs – Braes o' Mar – Jenny Dang The Weaver. The Cairding o't – The Lad Wi' the Plaidie – Fairy Dance.

The Society plays many sets that were either composed or arranged by John Robertson, a member of the Society. He conducted a group, which included other members of the Society, known as the Scottish Country Dance Players. They made sixteen 78 rpm records in 1948–49, most of them 'under the auspices of the Scottish Country Dance

Society': HMV B.9727–35, 9752, 9859, 9943, 9944; HMV C.3841–43.

In 1964, extracts from the Annual Concert were recorded but never released.

In 1976, the Society staged a Fiddlers' Rally in the Usher Hall with over 140 fiddlers on the platform. This concert was recorded and issued on LP and cassette:
The Scottish Fiddlers' Welcome to Edinburgh
Scottish Records – SR 141.

In 1977, another Fiddlers' Rally was recorded in the Usher Hall, for the International Gathering of the Clans, this time with over 160 fiddlers on the platform, and was issued on LP and cassette:
The Scottish Fiddlers' Welcome to the Clans
Scottish Records – SR 144.

On 3 December 1983, 'A Musical Evening with Regimental Bands and the Edinburgh Fiddlers' was staged in the Usher Hall. This concert was recorded live by Craighall Studio Production and was issued on LP:
In Concert with Combined Bands from The Scottish Division and The Edinburgh Fiddlers
ABF 101.

In 2000, George Robertson arranged for the older recordings of the Society, and the Scottish Country Dance Players, to be restored and archived on CD. Grateful thanks are due to Alan Bunting for the audio restoration.

The Reel Players

The Society is greatly indebted to 'The Reel Players' – they are the Society's link with the eighteenth century. Although they were not members of the Society, they were well known to, and taught, some of the early members including the 'brethren of the bow'.

William McLeish (the Aberfeldy Paganini).
Born in Aberfeldy in 1807. Taught by William Duncan and Alexander Mackenzie, he was an excellent fiddle player, composer and teacher. It was said his playing was 'neat and clean and free from rasp'. He taught both James Stewart Robertson (President) and William Simpson (Leader). Died in Aberfeldy in 1890.

James McIntosh.
Born in Dunkeld in 1791. He was the last pupil of Niel Gow, a bold and powerful player who composed many fine reels. Died in Edinburgh in 1877.

Robert Barclay Stewart.
Born in 1804. An excellent violinist and arranger, for many years connected with the leading concerts and balls given at Edinburgh. About 1857 he succeeded Alexander Mackenzie as leader of the Theatre Royal, Edinburgh. He taught William Simpson (Leader). Died in Edinburgh in 1885.

Robert Parry.
No information.

James Allan.
Born in Forfar in 1800. It was said his reel playing was 'the nearest approach to Niel Gow's style of playing'. Died in Forfar in 1877.

Archibald Menzies, kinsman to Archibald Menzies (Conductor).
Born in Dull, Perthshire, about 1806. One of the best strathspey and
reel players of his day, he invariably took first prize at competitions.
Willie Blair said 'he was a very clean player'. He played at the Theatre
Royal, Edinburgh for several years until his death. Died in Edinburgh in
1856.

Duncan McKerracher (the Athole Paganini).
Born in Inver in 1796. It was said his playing was characterised by
'considerable spirit and accent, but a hard rasp was always present'. He
taught James Stewart Robertson (President). Died in Edinburgh in
1873.

Index